THE FISH-TAILED MONSTER IN GREEK AND ETRUSCAN ART

THE FISH-TAILED MONSTER IN GREEK AND ETRUSCAN ART

BY KATHARINE SHEPARD

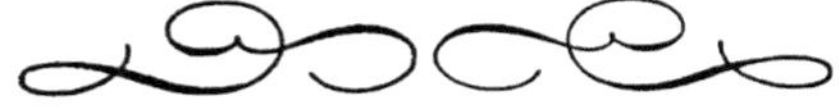

PRIVATELY PRINTED
NEW YORK : 1940

The Fish-Tailed Monster in Greek and Etruscan Art, by Katharine Shepard
First published 1940

CoachwhipBooks.com

ISBN 1-61646-074-1
ISBN-13 978-1-61646-074-7

Caeruleo per summa levis volat aequora curru;
subsident undae, tumidumque sub axe tonanti
sternitur aequor aquis; fugiunt vasto aethere nimbi.
Tum variae comitum facies, immania cete,
et senior Glauci chorus, Inousque Palaemon,
Tritonesque citi, Phorcique exercitus omnis;
laeva tenent Thetis, et Melite, Panopeaque virgo,
Nisaee, Spioque, Thaliaque, Cymodeceque.

Vergil, *Aeneid*, V, 819 ff.

PREFACE

My indebtedness to scholars who have dealt with this subject or parts of it has been indicated in the footnotes. I wish here to thank the museums that have given me permission to publish objects hitherto unpublished and the publishers who have given me permission to reproduce from their publications.

I am indebted to museum curators for permission to publish objects which have not been published before, as follows: to Dr. Moortgat of the Berlin Museum for the Assyrian relief shown in Fig. 6; to Mr. Bernard Ashmole of the British Museum for a Praenestine cista (Fig. 84); to Miss Gisela M. A. Richter of the Metropolitan Museum of Art for a black-figured hydria (Fig. 27); to Mr. L. D. Caskey of the Museum of Fine Arts Boston for an Etruscan bronze figure of Triton (Fig. 42), a Faliscan stamnos (Fig. 82) and an Apulian askos (Fig. 83); and to Mr. Morgan Marshall of the Walters Art Gallery, Baltimore, for a Greek marble vase (Fig. 62).

The following figures are reproduced by permission from various publishers: Fig. 3 from Baron von Oppenheim, *Der Tell Halaf*, F. A. Brockhaus, Leipzig; Figs. 17a, b and 18b from Humfry, Payne, *Necrocorinthia*, the Clarendon Press, Oxford; Fig. 48 a, b, c from Weege, *Etruskische Malerei*, Max Niemeyer, Halle; Fig. 71 from Beazley and Ashmole, *Greek Sculpture and Painting*, Cambridge University Press, the Macmillan Company; Fig. 72 from Guy Dickins, *Hellenistic Sculpture*, the Clarendon Press, Oxford; Figs. 97, 99 and 100 from Ducati, *Storia dell'Arte Etrusca*, Rinascimento del Libro, Florence.

Fig. 11 is reproduced from Payne, *Necrocorinthia*, the Clarendon Press, Oxford by courtesy of the Visitors of the Ashmolean Museum, Oxford, and Fig. 18a from the same book by the courtesy of Dr. Mayence of the Brussels Museum; Figs 36 and 54 from the *Corpus Vasorum Antiquorum*, British Museum, Édouard Champion, Paris with the permission of the Trustees of the British Museum; Fig. 58 from the *British Museum Catalogue of Coins, Crete and the Aegean Islands*, also with their permission. Professor D. M. Robinson has kindly allowed me to make use of the Nereid mosaic (Fig. 73) published by him in *Excavations at Olynthos*, the Johns Hopkins University Press, Baltimore, vols. II and V, and also the state seal of Larissa Kremaste in his private collection (Fig. 75) from the *American Journal of Archaeology*, 1934, pp. 219 ff.

Illustrations reproduced from other books and periodicals are as follows:

Fig. 1 from *Iraq* I, 1.

Fig. 2 from Ward, *Seal Cylinders of Western Asia.*

Fig. 4 from Ohnefalsch-Richter, *Kypros, the Bible and Homer.*

Figs. 8, 37, 59, 68, 77, 94 and 95 are from Imhoof-Blümer and Keller, *Tier- und Pflanzenbilder auf Münzen und Gemmen des klassischen Altertums.*

Figs. 9 and 39 from the *Annual of the British School at Athens.*

Fig. 10 from *Olympia,* IV.

Fig. 12 from Heuzey, *Les figurines antiques de terre cuite du Musée du Louvre.*

Figs. 13, 24, 25 and 87 from the *Athenische Mittheilungen.*

Figs. 14, 15, 40, 76, 86 and 93 from Furtwängler, *Die Antiken Gemmen.*

Fig. 16 from Furtwängler, "Der Goldfund von Vettersfelde," *Berliner Winckelmannsprogramm,* XLIII, 1883, pp. 25 ff.

Figs. 19, 63 and 74 from *The Illustrated London News.*

Figs. 20, 41 and 46 from *Antike Denkmäler.*

Fig. 21 from the *Papers of the British School at Rome.*

Figs. 22 and 35 from Ducati, *Pontische Vasen.*

Figs. 23, 45 and 50 from *Römische Mittheilungen.*

Fig. 26 from *Clara Rhodos.*

Fig. 29 from the *Annuario.*

Figs. 30, 33, 47 and 89 from the *Journal of Hellenic Studies.*

Fig. 31 from Perrot and Chipiez, *Histoire de l'art dans l'antiquité,* VI.

Fig. 32 from Ross, *Reisen auf den griechischen inseln des ägäischen* Meeres, III.

Figs. 38, 49, 79 and 80 from *Monumenti inediti dell'Instituto archeologico.*

Figs. 51 and 52 from Mühlestein, *Die Kunst der Etrusker, Die Ursprünge.*

Fig. 55 from *Annali dell'Instituto archeologico.*

Figs. 57, 60, 61, 64, 66 and 67 are from Jacobsthal, *Die melische Reliefs.*

Figs. 65, 75, 88 and 103 from the *American Journal of Archaeology.*

Fig. 78 from Langlotz, *Griechische Vasen in Würzburg.*

Fig. 81 from the *Corpus Vasorum Antiquorum,* Villa Giulia, III.

Fig. 85 from *Altertümer von Pergamum,* VII, 2.

Fig. 91 from the *Archäologische Anzeiger*.

Fig. 92 from Carapanos, *Dodone et ses ruines*.

Fig. 101 from the *Numismatic Chronicle*.

Exact references in all cases may be found in the footnotes. The remaining illustrations are taken from photographs.

K. S.

CONTENTS

INTRODUCTION

It has sometimes been mistakenly supposed that the gods of the Greeks were fixed forms throughout the course of Greek history. On the contrary (like the Old Man of the Sea) their forms were constantly changing to suit the varied and changing religious beliefs of the people.[1] As Wilamowitz points out, the gods lived only in belief.

The starting point of our study must naturally be the pre-Greek period, because not a few of the religious conceptions of the Hellenic people are inheritances from the Minoan-Mycenaean age.[2] The pre-Greek origin of certain Greek goddesses, such as Artemis and Athena, is easily proved by abundant monumental evidence.[3] Unfortunately, most of the Hellenic sea-deities are of obscure origin, but the possibility of a Minoan-Mycenaean prototype must be considered.

Although the cult of Poseidon is very old in Greece, it does not antedate the Hellenic period.[4] He was one of the deities brought down from the north by the invading people. In their northern home, where they had no close contact with the sea and no need for a sea-god, Poseidon was the earth-shaker. He presided over the underworld and had as his consort the earth goddess. In Greece, however, where the sea played an important part in the life of the people, he became the chief sea-deity. Who, then, were his predecessors? For it is inconceivable that the inhabitants of Greece were at any time without a sea-god.

A great maritime people like the Minoans must surely have had divinities who presided over the sea. There seem good reasons for believing that the Minoans had a polytheistic religion rather than the dual monotheism formerly ascribed to them.[5] As to the nature of their sea-divinities, monuments tell us nothing, unless the figure pictured in the boat on the gem from Mochlos is a sea-goddess.[6] Among the minor sea-divinities worshipped in Hellenic times, the goddess Ino almost certainly is of pre-Greek origin.[7] Her name seems to be connected with

[1] Wilamowitz-Moellendorff, *Der Glaube der Hellenen*, Berlin, 1931-1932, I, pp. 1 ff.

[2] Nilsson, *The Minoan-Mycenaen Religion and its Survival in Greek Religion*, Lund, 1927.

[3] *Ibid.*, pp. 415 ff.

[4] Wilamowitz, *op. cit.*, I, pp. 212 ff.

[5] Nilsson, *op. cit.*, pp. 334 ff.

[6] Seager, *Mochlos*, Boston and New York, 1912, Fig. 52.

[7] Wilamowitz, *op. cit.*, I, p. 102 and pp. 216 ff.

Inachos and Inopos. In legends she was identified with the Hellenic Leukothea. Her son was the Corinthian sea-god Palaimon, whose name means wrestler. Important features of the cult of Ino-Leukothea are the ritual leap and the association of mother and child, both of which may have reached Greece from Crete.[8] The cult of Palaimon appears to have been confined to Corinth. He was also called Melikertes, but the name does not belong in Corinth and had nothing to do with the cult.

In Hesiod's *Theogony* we find mentioned a number of sea-deities.[9] Okeanos was a Carian god who apparently supplanted the Hellenic Acheloos as a god of fresh water. Pontos, the father of Nereus, has no definite personality. The most important sea-gods for our purposes are Halios Geron and the group of deities connected with him. It seems probable that Halios Geron, the nameless Old Man of the Sea, was the principal pre-Hellenic sea-god and hence the predecessor of Poseidon. Evidence which will be discussed later shows that Halios Geron was originally a separate deity. As time went on, however, local gods with similar functions were identified with him. Of the gods associated with him, Glaukos is almost certainly Cretan and Triton is perhaps not Hellenic. Attempts to explain Phorkys as a Greek name are so unsatisfactory that we may assume that the name is also pre-Hellenic. It seems probable also that the deities Taras and Phalanthos, associated in legends with the founding of Tarentum in Southern Italy, are of pre-Greek origin. They are dolphin-riders and the dolphin-god may also be Cretan.

The three most important types of fish-tailed monsters, the merman, the hippocamp and the *ketos*, all appear on Greek monuments of the Orientalizing period. Although we are able to prove only in the case of the merman a direct borrowing from the East, the early examples of the other two types have a decidedly Oriental appearance. These types continued to be used in Greek art after the decline of Oriental influence, but in the fifth century they were comparatively rare. The mermen of the fifth century are usually clothed and act as companions and servants to the sea-deities. The fish-tail has become more insignificant than in the seventh- and sixth-century types.

Both the hippocamp and the *ketos* occur but seldom on monuments of the fifth century. To the first half of the fifth century, however, belong the earliest monuments which represent Nereids riding sea-

[8] The leap may have come to Crete from the East. See Chap. I, n. 23.

[9] *Theogony*, pp. 233 ff. Cf. Wilamowitz, *op. cit.*, I, p. 219.

monsters and carrying the weapons of Achilles. Thus it is established beyond doubt that Skopas was not the inventor of such types, as scholars earlier believed. It is probable, however, that the famous group of Skopas, described by Pliny, had much to do with the popularity of Nereids on sea-monsters in the Hellenistic age.

Examples of the Skylla type appear for the first time in the fifth century. She is represented as a much humanized mermaid with the foreparts of dogs joined to her waist or shoulders.

The sea-monsters of the Hellenistic age are more difficult to explain. The Greeks of this period did not restrict themselves to three or four fixed types, but freely used all sorts of combinations. Many of the figures have a very bizarre appearance, with leafy girdles and long serpentine tails. It would certainly seem that one great work, such as that of Skopas, must have influenced these types. The mermen are often pictured as youthful and beardless and any number of them may be represented on the same monument. A very large number of sea-monsters of the Hellenistic period carry Nereids on their backs. Very often the maidens bear weapons, but just as often they have other objects such as wine cups and baskets of fruit. Possibly these sea thiasoi are symbolic of the passage of the dead over the sea to the West—a subject which would appeal especially to the Greeks in an age of heroization and deification. Belief in an individual after-life, although denied at this time by many of the philosophers was adhered to by the common people.[10] The cult of the dead persisted. Deification, an idea foreign to the Greek mind, was introduced by Alexander the Great.

The Roman sea-monsters, for the most part, represent a borrowing from the Greek. A large number occur on Roman sarcophagi. These doubtless also symbolize the journey of the dead to the Hereafter. Figures of sea-monsters were also often used in the mosaic patterns of Roman baths, but here the motifs are purely decorative.

The frequency of sea-monsters in Etruscan art as compared with Greek is very striking. This is especially true in the archaic period, when the hippocamp type was rare on Greek monuments, but common on Etruscan. The occurrence of sea-monsters on Etruscan tomb paintings, cinerary urns and sarcophagi indicates that here also they were probably symbolic of the passage of the dead to a future life. The Etruscans often copied the Greek types, but they had besides many curious monsters of their own invention.

[10] Wilamowitz, *op. cit.*, II, pp. 313 ff.

I

THE FISH-TAILED MONSTER IN THE ORIENT

It is a well-known fact that many hybrid monsters such as gryphons, dragons and certain types of winged human beings originated in the Orient and that when they occur in Greek art they are borrowed from the East.[1] This is the case even with the centaur, so familiar in the mythology and art of Greece. Since there was such a predilection for fabulous creatures in the Orient, it is only natural to seek there the prototype of the fish-tailed monster which came to Greece in the seventh century and which was in use until late Roman times. Indeed, the form of the fish-god Triton was long ago derived from the Orient: in 1879 Furtwängler brought forward this view[2] and his opinion has been generally accepted by scholars.[3]

Among the earliest Oriental monuments which have been thought to be decorated with representations of a fish-tailed monster are a number of ancient Babylonian seal cylinders, dated about 3000-2700 B.C. Some of these appear to show a monster with human head and arms and a long fishlike tail; others seem to picture a boat with the prow in the form of a man and with a fish-tail for the stern.[4] Frankfort's recent discoveries at Tell Asmar and Khafaje, however, definitely prove that we are not dealing with a sea-monster, but with the boat of the sun in

[1] Cf. Unger, "Mischwesen", in Ebert's *Reallexikon der Vorgeschichte*, for the Oriental types.

[2] "Die Bronzefunde aus Olympia", *Abh. d. K. Wiss. zu Berlin*, 1879, p. 98. Cf. "Der Goldfund von Vettersfelde", *Berliner Winckelmannsprogramm*, XLIII, 1883, p. 25.

[3] Dressler, *Triton und die Tritonen in der Literatur und Kunst der Griechen und Römer*, Gymnasium-Programm, Wurzen, 1892-1893, pt. I, pp. 15 ff.; Escher, *Triton und seine Bekämpfung durch Herakles*, Leipzig, 1890, p. 111. Vs. this view cf. von Wahl, *Quomodo monstra marina artifices Graeci finxerint, capita selecta*, Bonn, 1896, pp. 8 ff. He argues that "Triton" was an invention of the Ionic Greeks.

[4] Ward, *Seal Cylinders of Western Asia*, Washington, 1910, pp. 41-42, Figs. 105-109; by the same author, *Cylinders and other Ancient Oriental Seals in the Library of J. P. Morgan*, New York, 1909, nos. 7-8. Cf. *Illustrated London News*, July 15, 1933, p. 99, second seal, third row (Frankfort). Here a boat is definitely seen with a prow and a fish-tail. Ward accepts both possibilities—a boat in human form in some instances and a composite creature in others.

semi-human form.[5] Sometimes the stern ends in an ear of corn instead of a serpent body (Fig. 1).

Many well-attested later examples of the man-fish or merman are found in Oriental art of the second half of the third millenium. A seal cylinder of the time of Gudea (*ca.* 2450) pictures Ea standing on a man-fish and a goat-fish, the prototype of the later Capricorn (Fig. 2).[6] Another example of the man-fish occurs on an Elamite stele of about 1500 B.C. where a beardless deity is depicted whose lower body, covered with scales, ends in the tail of a fish.[7] Further, the handle of a silver sceptre, decorated with friezes like a seal cylinder, shows a sphinx in combat with a merman.[8] The sceptre belongs to the Syro-Hittite culture of about 2000 B.C. In addition, a Hittite conoid seal, perhaps as early as 1100 B.C., has the interesting design of two human-headed sea-monsters rampant and crossed.[9] A well-preserved example of a genuine fish-tailed monster is also found on a Subaraean relief recently excavated at Tell Halaf by Baron von Oppenheim.[10] This bearded deity with a scaly fish body is represented in Fig. 3.

Aside from these very early specimens of the man-fish, the type is also found on Assyrian monuments. A fish-tailed deity on a well-known relief from Sargon's palace has been generally associated with the Philistine god, Dagon, of whom no certain representation exists, but who may have had the form of a merman (Fig. 4).[11] The name Dagon may be connected with the Hebrew word for "fish", and this derivation has given rise to the idea that the god was represented as a merman. The well-attested worship of fish deities in Syria also favors the derivation of the word Dagon from "fish". It is possible, however, that Philo of Byblos, who derived the name from the Hebrew word for "grain", is correct, as many scholars believe.[12] The probability of a relationship

[5] Frankfort, *Iraq*, I, 1, pp. 18 ff. and Pl. III, e-g; *Oriental Institute Communications*, no. 17, p. 53, Fig. 49. Cf. also Fig. 48.

[6] Ward, *Seal Cylinders of Western Asia*, p. 214, Fig. 649.

[7] Contenau, *Les Antiquités orientales du Musée National du Louvre: Sumer, Babylonie, Élam*, Paris, 1927, no. 52, fragment A; *Rev. d'Assyr.*, XIII, 1916, pp. 119-124 (Pézard).

[8] Weber, *Jahrbuch der preuszischen Kunstsammlungen*, 1916, pp. 52 ff., Fig. 1. Cf. n. 1 above. Unger believes this monster to be female.

[9] Hogarth, *Hittite Seals with Particular Reference to the Ashmolean Collection*, Oxford, 1920, Pl. IX, no. 275 and p. 86.

[10] von Oppenheim, *Der Tell Halaf*, Leipzig, 1931, p. 155 and Fig. 35b.

[11] Botta-Flandin, *Monuments de Ninive découverts et décrits*, Paris, 1848, I, Pl. 32; Ohnefalsch-Richter, *Kypros, the Bible and Homer*, London, 1893, Pl. 97, Fig. 3.

[12] Müller, *Frm. Hist. Gr.*, III, p. 567, Frm. 2, 14 ff.

with the Assyrian god, Dagan, cannot help us here, as very little is known of his character. It is tempting to connect Dagan with 'Ωδάκων, one of the monsters, part man and part fish, whom Berosos mentions as coming up from the Erythraean Sea at long intervals to repeat to the Chaldaeans the revelation of Oannes.[13] This deity, as we shall see later, wears the fish-skin cloak and is quite different from the ordinary merman. Some Phoenician coins of Arados of the late fifth and fourth centuries have on the obverse a deity in the form of a merman.[14] He is often called Dagon, but he holds a dolphin and a wreath—attributes of the Greek "Triton". Coins of such late date tell us nothing of the origin of the type.[15] They are interesting in that they show a continued predilection for the fish type.

Mermen, often antithetically grouped, occur on a number of Assyrian cone seals. The fish part has a straight tail and in many cases an angular joining of the human and fish bodies.[16] The unfishlike bend in the body of the Assyrian monster is unique and differs so greatly from the curving lines of the Greek divinity, "Triton", that some authorities believe the Greeks did not derive the "Triton" type from the Orient but invented it. The Greeks, however, might well have taken the idea from the East and modified it to suit themselves.

Another kind of fish deity, fairly frequent on Assyrian monuments, is the god who wears the fish-skin cloak with the head of a fish over his head and the tail reaching down his back. The passage in Berosos referred to above, describes the god Oannes who issued from the Erythraean Sea and taught the Chaldaeans science and the fine arts.[17] Berosos relates that Oannes had the body of a fish, but that under the head of the fish was the head of a man and the man had human feet. This type is found on a copper plaque of the eighth or seventh century B.C. (Fig. 5).[17a] Because of the passage in Berosos, Assyrian representa-

[13] *Ibid.*, II, p. 496, Frm. 1, 3.

[14] *Brit. Mus. Cat. Coins, Phoenicia* (Hill), London, 1910, pp. 1-3, 12. Dagon has also been identified with the Phoenician sun-god, Melqart (Dussaud, *Rev. Arch.*, III, 1904, pp. 210 ff.). Babelon, *Traité des monnaies grecques et romaines*, pt. 2, vol. II, Paris, 1910, pp. 511 ff.

[15] Dussaud (*Revue de l'Histoire des Religions*, 103-105, 1932, p. 264) believes that the figure may be a representation of Aleiyan Ba'al.

[16] Delaporte, *Catalogue des cylindres orientaux et des cachets assyro-babyloniens, perses et syro-cappadociens de la Bibliothèque Nationale*, Paris, 1910, nos. 540a, 543a; Lajard, *Recherches sur le culte de Mithras*, Paris, 1847, Pls. LXII, 1, 2a; XVII, 2b.

[17] Cf. n. 13 above.

[17a] Thureau-Dangin, *Rev. d'Assyr.*, XVIII, 1921, pp. 173 and 189 ff.

tions of the type have usually been associated with Oannes. The monster occurs on a number of Babylonian and Assyrian seal cylinders and cone seals of the first millennium B.C., where the deity is shown engaged in some sort of sacrifice in connection with the sacred tree.[18] The type is found in the same connection on an Assyrian relief in Berlin of the eighth or seventh century B.C. (Fig. 6). In the palace of Kouyunjik two colossal doorways are decorated with bas-reliefs of figures wearing the fish-skin cloak, supposedly representations of Oannes.[19] The upper part of the figures is destroyed.

We may infer from literary accounts relating to the Phoenician goddess, Derketo, that the mermaid type existed in the Orient, but there are no absolutely certain representations of her. A bronze statuette has been found in Palestine which seems to represent a creature with the head and body of a woman and the tail of a fish.[20] The goddess Nina, the daughter of Ea, may have been thought of as a mermaid. In the song of Nina, there are references to fish combinations such as the bull-fish, the bird-fish and the fish-cloak.[21] The goddess Derketo was sometimes worshipped in Syria in the form of a mermaid. Diodoros relates that Aphrodite, enraged at Derketo, caused her to fall in love with a mortal.[22] After giving birth to a child, she jumped into the sea and became a mermaid.[23] In regard to this divinity, Lucian says: "Now I have seen the semblance of Derketo in Phoenicia and a wonderful sight it is; one half is a woman, but the part which extends from the thighs to the feet ends in a fish's tail. The effigy, however, which is at Hierapolis, is a complete woman. The reasons for this story are plain to understand; they deem fishes holy objects and never touch them".[24] It is barely possible that we have a representation of Derketo in the Palestinian statuette mentioned above. The tradition of a fish-tailed goddess seems to have lingered at Hierapolis, since two late writers, Maundrell in 1697, and another author in 1745, mention a well, carved with the figures of "syrens", making a seat for a woman with their fishy tails.[25]

[18] Delaporte, *op. cit.*, nos. 384, 541, 555c, 566b; Lajard, *op. cit.*, Pl. XVII, nos. 1, 3, 5, 8; Pl. XVI, no. 7a; Roscher's *Lexikon*, s.v. "Oannes", Figs. 2 ff.

[19] Layard, *Nineveh and Babylon*, London, 1853, pp. 343 and 350.

[20] Bliss and Macalister, *Excavations in Palestine*, London, 1902, p. 148, Fig. 60.

[21] Scheil, *Rev. d'Assyr.*, XV, 1918, pp. 127 ff., and p. 132, Figs. 1-5.

[22] Diodoros, II, 4.

[23] This may point to an Eastern origin for the ritual leap which we find later in Crete. There is, however, the possibility that it may have gone the other way.

[24] *De Dea Syria*, 14. Translation from Garstang and Strong, *The Syrian Goddess*, London, 1913, pp. 52 ff.

[25] *Ibid.*, pp. 91-93.

Non-human types were also found in Oriental art, especially the goat-fish or Capricorn, which as the symbol of the water god Ea, occurs on many monuments (Fig. 7).[25a] This type was apparently not used by the Greeks except in the Hellenistic age.[26] In the Roman period, however, we find it on coins, particularly in Asia Minor (Fig. 8).[27] Of special interest are two winged monsters represented on a Hittite seal cylinder of about 2000 B.C. One has the head of a dog attached to a fish body; the other the head and body of a dog, the legs of a bull and the tail of a fish.[28] These at once call to mind the Greek *ketos* or sea-dragon, with its doglike head. A connection, however, cannot be proved, though the appearance of the *ketos* in Crete may give us the link between the Orient and Greece. There are a few instances in Oriental art of other fish combinations, such as the sea-bull[29] and the sea-lion.[30] Although there are examples of all these types on Hellenistic and Roman monuments, they may have been invented in the Hellenistic age rather than borrowed from the East.

Evidence appears to point to the creation in the Orient at an early date of the merman, the mermaid, the god with the fish-skin cloak and numerous non-human types, such as the goat-fish, the sea-lion, bird-fish, dog-headed fish and sea-bull. When one considers the great variety of fish-tailed monsters which existed in Oriental art, the absence of the hippocamp is striking. This monster appeared in Greek art during the period of Oriental influence, and it would be natural to suppose that, like the man-fish and other hybrid types, the hippocamp was also derived from the East. Up to the present, however, no examples have been discovered there. The epic of Aleiyan Ba'al, which is dated about 1400 B.C., possibly gives us the literary prototype of the hippocamp in Phoenicia. The god Kousor, the brother of Aleiyan, is here described as

[25a] Kassite boundary stone in the Louvre, Contenau, *op. cit.*, Pl. 36.

[26] Walters, *Catalogue of the Engraved Gems and Cameos, Greek, Roman and Etruscan in the British Museum*, London, 1926 (hereafter referred to as *Brit. Mus. Cat. Gems*), no. 1205. Capricorn had a connection with Crete. See Robert, *Erat. Katasterism.*, Frm. 148 ff. Cf. also Lehmann-Hartleben, *Röm. Mitt.*, XLII, pp. 169 ff.

[27] *Brit. Mus. Cat. Coins, Pontus, etc.* (Wroth), p. 22, no. 88, and p. 182, no. 18; *ibid., Ionia* (Head), p. 267, no. 253; Imhoof-Blümer and Keller, *Tier- und Pflanzenbilder auf Münzen und Gemmen des klassischen Altertums*, Leipzig, 1889 (hereafter referred to as I.-B. and K.), Pl. XI, nos. 1-3.

[28] Weber, *op. cit.*, Fig. 27 (Collection de Clercq, no. 365).

[29] Scheil, *Rev. d'Assyr.*, 1918, p. 132.

[30] Delaporte, *Catalogue des cylindres, cachets, et pierres gravées du style oriental du Musée National du Louvre*, II, Paris, 1923, Pl. 80, Fig. 12, and Pl. 78, Fig. 18 (sea-lion and sea-dog).

driving a chariot over the sea and commanding his chargers to push the water against the throne of Ba'al. The poems were composed in Phoenicia and represent the sea beating furiously against the island of Tyre.[31]

An examination of the fish-tailed deities in the Orient leads to the conclusion that the Greeks derived their notions of such divinities from the East. The derivation of the man-fish is obvious. The occurrence, however, of some of the same types on both Oriental and late Greek monuments may be mere coincidence.

It seems probable that the Greeks took over from the Orient their stories of sea-monsters as well as the fish-tailed forms in art. The Phoenicians, who were pioneers in maritime trade in the Mediterranean, would have had stories to tell to credulous natives. Thus the legend of Skylla and Charybdis, of the hero wrestling with a sea-divinity and possibly also of Perseus and Andromeda became part of Greek mythology. The borrowing from the East may even have begun in the Minoan period if certain monuments have been interpreted correctly (cf. Fig. 39 and pp. 28, 43 ff.

[31] See Dussaud, "Les éléments déchaînés", *Syria,* XVI, 1935, p. 199, 11. Cf. also Dussaud, *Revue de l'Histoire des Religions,* 105-106, 1932, pp. 264 ff. Poseidon is represented on coins of Beirut driving a quadriga of hippocamps. Melqart riding a hippocamp appears on Tyrian coins from the late fifth century onward (cf. Babelon, *op. cit.,* pp. 615 ff. See also Fig. 37b). The hippocamp is also found on coins of Arados under the galley represented on the reverse (see p. 7 and Babelon, *op. cit.,* pp. 511 ff. and Hill, *op. cit.,* pp. 2-3). A similar type occurs at Byblos (Babelon, *op. cit.,* p. 535). Cf. Chap. IV, n. 29. A letter discovered by Schaeffer in the most recent campaign or Ras Shamra fixes the date of the epic at ca. 1400 B.C. (cf. *Syria,* 1939, p. 171). It may have been transmitted orally for centuries but it cannot have assumed anything like its present form before the seventeenth century B.C. I owe this information to Dr. Albright of Johns Hopkins University.

II

SEA-MONSTERS IN ARCHAIC GREEK ART

We should naturally expect to find that sites closely in touch with the Orient would furnish our earliest examples of sea-monsters. As a matter of fact, we have few specimens from such sites and most of these not earlier than the sixth century. Crete offers only the seventh-century plate from Praesos, which may represent a hero wrestling with a sea-divinity; or a dolphin-rider (Fig. 9), although neither of these interpretations can be proved.[1] It is disappointing to find that Cyprus, in spite of its close relations with the East, has given us very few examples of sea-monsters. Ohnefalsch-Richter assumed the worship of Dagon in Cyprus, but on somewhat slender evidence.[2] One gem of the sixth century has a hippocamp as a design—the earliest Greek monument from Cyprus known to me with a representation of a sea-monster.[3] The case appears to be similar with Rhodes. There is only an ivory relief of the sixth century with a carving of a fish-tailed "siren" from Rhodes (Fig. 29).[4] Melos is somewhat more promising, but with less than a dozen examples of Island gems. On these are found designs of the man-fish and hippocamp. Besides the islands, the centers where these monsters occur are Ionia, Corinth, Attica and Etruria—sites with important Eastern connections.

The most common type of sea-monster in archaic Greek art is the man-fish or merman. Like their Oriental forebears, the archaic mermen have the joining of the fish body with the human form just below the chest. Both the nude and clothed types occur. The figures are always bearded.

The oldest inscribed example of this type, found on a bronze plaque from Olympia, bears the name Halios Geron (Fig. 10).[5] He was probably a pre-Hellenic sea-divinity, worshipped rather generally through-

[1] Hopkinson, *B.S.A.*, X, 1904, pp. 149 ff. and pl. 3; cf. also for Theseus legend as a possible theme here, G. W. Elderkin, *A.J.A.*, XIV, 1910, pp. 190-192.

[2] Ohnefalsch-Richter, *op. cit.*, pp. 287-290.

[3] Myres, *Handbook of the Cesnola Collection of Antiquities from Cyprus*, New York, 1914, p. 419, no. 4194. For illustration see Cesnola, *Cyprus*, New York, 1878, Pl. 40, no. 18.

[4] Maiuri, *Annuario*, VI-VII, pp. 322 ff. and Fig. 216A.

[5] Furtwängler, "Die Bronzefunde aus Olympia", pp. 96 ff. and *Olympia*, IV, Berlin, 1890, pp. 101 ff., no. 699a and Pl. XXXIX (Athens).

out Greece. There are good reasons for believing that he was originally quite distinct from Nereus, Proteus, Phorkys, Triton and Glaukos, who were all more or less identified with him later.

The earliest literary references to Halios Geron are in Homer. Thetis is described several times as *θυγάτηρ ἁλίοιο γέροντος*[6] and her sisters are *κοῦραι ἁλίοιο γέροντος.*[7] Although the name Nereus is never used in Homer, the maidens are called Nereids in the *Iliad.*[8] This would seem to show that the identification of Nereus with Halios Geron had already taken place at this time.[9] The notion of the Old Man of the Sea and his daughters, the sea-maidens, was undoubtedly much older.[10] In Hesiod the identification is more firmly established. Nereus is qualified, *ὅν καλέουσι γέροντα,* and the sea-maidens *Νηρῆος κοῦραι ἁλίοιο γέροντος.*[11] The separate personality of Halios Geron, however, persisted in some localities for hundreds of years. Pausanias mentions the worship of Geron at Gytheion in Laconia and identifies the god with Nereus, probably because Nereus was familiar to him.[12] The scholiast on Apollonios Rhodios speaks of a shrine to Geron in Iberia.[13] He is in this passage identified with Glaukos, but a Latin reference indicates that *Γλαύκου* was probably substituted for *γέροντος.*[14] Dionysios of Byzantium gives some information concerning a cult of Halios Geron at Byzantium.[15] The deity was variously identified at that time with Nereus, Phorkys, Proteus and the father of Semestra, a local nymph. There was also a tradition that he showed the Argonauts the way through the narrows.

We have two authentic representations of Halios Geron in Greek art. The first is found on the Argive-Corinthian bronze relief from Olympia, just mentioned, showing Herakles in combat with a man-fish

[6] *Iliad,* I, 538, 556; XX, 107; XXIV, 562.

[7] *Odyssey,* XXIV, 58.

[8] Several times in the beginning of *Iliad,* XVIII.

[9] Kourouniotis in his dissertation, *Herakles mit Halios Geron und Triton auf Werken der altertümlichen griechischen Kunst,* Munich, 1893, advances the opinion that the name *Nereid* is older than *Nereus* and that Nereus was invented later, perhaps by Hesiod, to furnish a genealogy for the family. The objection to this theory is that *Nereid* is a patronymic form.

[10] Wilamowitz, *op. cit.,* I, pp. 219 ff.

[11] *Theogony,* 234 and 1003.

[12] Pausanias, III, 21, 9.

[13] Schol. on Apol. Rh., II, 767.

[14] Avienus, *Ora Maritima,* 263 ff.

[15] *De Bospori Navigatione,* pp. 19-20 (ed. Wescher).

(Fig. 10).[16] On the relief is a retrograde inscription in the Argive alphabet, which Furtwängler restored as Ἡρακλῆς and ἅλιος γέρων. The same subject matter is found on a large number of black-figured vases, where the name of the monster, however, is given as Triton. The other certified example of Halios Geron occurs on a black-figured vase by the painter, Kolchos.[17] Here the deity at the extreme left labeled Halios Geron is represented as a bearded old man wearing a long chiton and mantle. He is merely a human spectator of the combat between Herakles and Kyknos. In appearance he is not unlike the figures of Nereus on the François and other black-figured vases and may not have been distinguished from him in the minds of the vase-painters.[17a] Of these two monuments depicting Halios Geron the relief is slightly older. It is usually dated about 570 B.C., whereas the vase belongs approximately in the middle of the sixth century.

In Hesiod, Nereus takes the place of Halios Geron as the father of the Nereids, but retains the title Halios Geron. The mother of the maidens is Doris, the daughter of Okeanos. This is probably genealogical invention on the part of Hesiod. No mother is mentioned in Homer. The characterization of Nereus comes mostly from the lines in *Theogony*, 233 ff.

> Νηρέα δ'ἀψευδέα καὶ ἀληθέα γείνατο Πόντος,
> πρεσβύτατον παίδων· αὐτὰρ καλέουσι γέροντα
> οὕνεκα νημερτής τε καὶ ἤπιος, οὐδὲ θεμιστέων
> λήθεται, ἀλλὰ δίκαια καὶ ἤπια δήνεα οἶδεν.

Such words as ἀψευδής and νημερτής lead us to assume that he had the gift of prophecy. He is called εὔβουλος by Pindar and Bacchylides.[18] The scholiast on Apollonios Rhodios quotes Pherekydes' account of the fight

[16] See above n. 5. The motive may be Eastern. Cf. prototype of Herakles in combat with the Hydra, *Illustr. London News*, July 22, 1933, pp. 124 ff. (Frankfort). Also *Oriental Institute Communication*, no. 17, p. 49 and Fig. 43.

[17] Gerhard, *Auserlesene Vasenbilder*, Berlin, 1840-1858, Pls. 122-123. *Wiener Vorlegeblätter*, 1889, Pl. II, 1. This vase is in Berlin.

[17a] On the François vase (Furtwängler-Reichhold, *Griechische Vasenmalerei*, Berlin, 1900-date, Pl. I) a figure of an old man is designated as Nereus. See Buschor, *Ath. Mitt.*, 1922, pp. 57 ff. It seems hardly safe to assume that the figure behind the chariot of Okeanos was certainly Triton. It is also possible that the fish-tailed monster on the Sophilos deinos was a hippocamp and not Triton (Graef, *Die antiken Vasen von der Akropolis zu Athen*, Berlin, 1909-1925, no. 587h and Pl. 26). Buschor is probably right, however, in saying that the functions of Halios Geron were divided between Nereus and Triton at this time.

[18] Pindar, *Pyth.*, III, 93. Bacchylides, Frm. 6 (ed. Kenyon, p. 199).

between Herakles and Nereus.[19] According to this narrative, Nereus changed himself first to fire and then to water in his efforts to escape, but finally gave up and in his natural shape imparted to Herakles the desired information concerning the golden apples. We learn from a later writer that Stesichoros described the changes of Nereus.[20] If he told the entire story, as seems probable, the literary tradition of the contest goes back at least to the middle of the sixth century. Mr. Luce ignores Stesichoros and Pherekydes and believes that Nereus was not attached to any such story before the time of Apollodoros.[21]

Nereus is frequently seen among the spectators on vases which picture the combat between Herakles and the fish-god, Triton. The identification is certain from inscriptions on two examples.[22] The interesting thing about these designs is that Nereus is not shown as a merman. As a dignified old man, white-haired and bearded, he wears a long chiton and carries a staff or sceptre. He resembles the uninscribed clothed figure, commonly called Nereus, who is shown in combat with Herakles on two black-figured vases.[23] It is impossible to identify this uninscribed figure with certainty. Mr. Luce believes that these vases show Herakles and Halios Geron, not Herakles and Nereus, and he may be right.[24] But, since the story of Herakles and Nereus probably goes back at least to the sixth century B.C., there is no reason why the contest should not have been represented on black-figured vases. Further, on both the vases in question there are indications of a marine setting which make certain the character of the divinity. On the second example, the vase in the Bibliothèque Nationale, are red lines indicating one of the metamorphoses of Nereus. Other changes are suggested on the same vase by the lion and the panther which the Nereids hold.

It appears, then, that Nereus developed out of the more ancient deity Halios Geron. Besides being the father of the Nereids in early literature, Nereus was also identical with the marine divinity who fought with Herakles. But he is not pictured as a fish-tailed deity in Greek art.[25] He

[19] Müller, *Frm. Hist. Gr.*, I, p. 79, Frm. 33 (Schol. on Apoll. Rh., IV, 1396).

[20] Keller, *Rerum Naturalium Scriptores Graeci Minores*, Leipzig, 1887, p. 110.

[21] Apollodoros, *Bibliotheca*, II, 5, 11. Cf. Luce *A.J.A.*, 1922, pp. 174 ff.

[22] a. Walters, *Catalogue of the Vases in the British Museum*, London, 1893-1925 (hereafter referred to as *Brit. Mus. Cat. Vases*), II, B 223, p. 21, Fig. 29. Also *J. H. S.*, XXVI, 1906, p. 15, Fig. 6.

b. Pottier, *Vases antiques du Louvre*, Paris, 1897-1922, II, F 298, Pl. 84.

[23] a. *C.V.A.*, Brit. Mus., III, III He, Pl. 55, 3a. *Brit. Mus. Cat. Vases*, II, B 225.

b. *C.V.A.*, Bibl. Nat., II, III He, Pl. 58, 6. Also Gerhard, *op. cit.*, Pl. 112.

[24] *A.J.A.*, XXVI, 1922, pp. 174 ff.

[25] Panofka believed he saw an inscription *Nereus* on a late red-figured vase

is frequently a spectator in the contest in which literature makes him a protagonist who changes his form.

The god Triton is not mentioned in Homer. The earliest reference to him is in Hesiod where he is described as δεινὸς θεός, the son of Poseidon and Amphitrite and an inhabitant of their golden house under the sea.[26] There is no mention of his fish-tailed form before the *Argonautika* of Apollonios Rhodios.[27] The earliest version of Triton and the Argonauts occurs in Herodotus, where he appears in the character of a seer.[28] The story is greatly amplified by Apollonios who relates how Triton changed from a young man into his more usual form of a merman. This is the only literary passage in which the god shows the power of metamorphosis. Pausanias, in discussing the headless Triton of Tanagra, pauses to describe the more normal form of the god. His Triton with gills and exaggerated mouth is a more monstrous creature than we are accustomed to see on Greek monuments.[29] Literature appears to emphasize his dread aspect as an inhabitant of the sea, dangerous for men. Evidence from literature and art makes us locate Triton in Attica and Boeotia.

On a large number of black-figured vases Herakles wrestles with a man-fish, designated by inscriptions as Triton.[30] No such contest is mentioned in literature. The combat between Herakles and the man-fish is a common subject in archaic Greek art and was doubtless suggested by the contests between men and monsters depicted on Oriental monuments. On these vases the Greek artists have given the name Triton to the opponent of Herakles, earlier known as Halios Geron.

To my knowledge, Triton is never represented in art except as a merman. That he was the most popular fish-deity in Greece, inscriptions on black- and red-figured vases prove. His name became a generic term.

(*Brit. Mus. Cat. Vases*, III, E 109); Lenormant-deWitte, *Élite des monuments céramographiques*, Paris, 1844-1866, III, Pl. 33), but Sir Cecil Smith does not think he was justified. Mr. Hinks of the British Museum was kind enough to examine the vase for me and he agrees with Sir Cecil Smith.

[26] *Theogony*, 930 ff.

[27] IV, 1610 ff.

[28] Herodotus, IV, 179.

[29] Pausanias, IX, 21, 1.

[30] a. n. 22a.

b. n. 22b.

c. *C.V.A.*, Cambridge I (Fitzwilliam Museum), III He, Pl. 16, 2; E. A. Gardner, *Catalogue of the Vases in the Fitzwilliam Museum*, Cambridge, 1897, Pl. 16.

d. G. von Lücken, *Griechische Vasenbilder*, Berlin, 1921, Pl. 2.

In later Greek and Roman art more than one Triton was often used on the same monument.

Two deities besides Nereus are given the name Halios Geron as a secondary title. The first is Proteus, with whom Menelaos wrestles in Egypt.[31] The details of the narrative resemble very closely the story of Herakles and Nereus as told by Pherekydes. Like Nereus, Proteus changes his form several times and is very reluctant to give information. It seems probable that originally there was one legend of a hero wrestling with a sea-monster. This was the opinion of von Duhn, who believed that in the original story Menelaos fought with a nameless Old Man of the Sea on some unknown island. The name Proteus and the localization in Egypt were a later interpolation.[32] In Herodotus, Proteus is the name of an Egyptian king.[33] In other accounts, however, Proteus is associated with Greece, particularly with Chalkis and Chalkidike. As in the case of certain legends of Boeotia and Euboea, the foreign connection is later and secondary.

The god Phorkys is twice called Halios Geron in Homer.[34] The meaning of the name, Phorkys, is very uncertain and none of the explanations gives satisfaction.[35] He was the father of many monsters. He is first mentioned in the *Odyssey* as the father of Thoosa, the mother of the Cyclops.[36] Usually, though not in Homer, he is the father of Skylla. Hesiod includes among his children the Graiai and the Gorgons.[37] Other authorities make him the father of the Sirens, Echidna and the Hesperides. To judge from his offspring, he was in all likelihood a monster himself. According to one author he had the power of changing his form like Nereus and Proteus.[38] There is no authentic representation of this deity in early art.[39] Pliny, along with the Tritons of Skopas' group, mentions a chorus Phorci.[40]

The last deity of the Halios Geron circle is Glaukos, who, like Triton,

[31] *Odyssey*, IV, 365 ff.

[32] von Duhn, *De Menelai Itinere Aegyptio*, Bonn, 1874, pp. 15 ff.

[33] Herodotus, II, 112 ff.

[34] *Odyssey*, XIII, 96 and 345.

[35] Roscher's *Lexikon*, s.v. "Phorkys".

[36] *Odyssey*, I, 71.

[37] *Theogony*, 270 ff. and 333 ff.

[38] Artemidoros, *Oneirocritica*, 2, 38.

[39] Cf. Campbell, "Excavations at Antioch-on-the-Orontes", *A.J.A.*, 1934, p. 205, and Pl. XXIV A. On the mosaic pavement here described there is a figure of a man-fish labeled *Phorkys*. This late Roman pavement done after the Hellenistic tradition is, so far as I know, the only certain representation of Phorkys.

[40] *N.H.*, XXXVI, 26.

is nowhere specifically called Halios Geron. In Hellenic times the center of his worship was Boeotia, particularly Anthedon, where he was prominent in local legends. Some scholars believe his cult goes back to Crete. In the first place, the name Anthedon with the -νθ combination belongs to a pre-Greek language. Secondly, his mother, Halkyone, and Pasiphae, the mother of Glaukos of Crete, were both daughters of Atlas and closely related. Thirdly, the name Glaukos was firmly rooted in Asia Minor, a center of pre-Greek culture with important Cretan connections. We have the mention of Glaukos of Lycia, the son or grandson of Bellerophon, commander with Sarpedon of the Lycian troops at Troy. The earliest references to the sea-god, Glaukos, are in Pindar and Aischylos. Although well-known as a warrior and as a lover, Glaukos was most famous as a soothsayer. Acting as spokesman of Nereus he prophesied to Menelaos at Malea and to the Argonauts during their voyage.[41] Some scholars have wished to identify many figures on coins and vases with Glaukos, but no authentic representation of him exists. Writers refer to him variously as κῆτος and ἀνθρωποειδες θηρίον, which indicates that he was a fish-formed deity. *Ketos* is used in general of a dog-headed sea-monster, as we shall see later. If Glaukos is a Cretan-Mycenaean inheritance, it is possible that the fish-tailed deities on the coins of Itanos represent this divinity (Fig. 58).[42] Some have suggested that the snake- and fish-tailed deities on Boeotian and Corinthian vases may also be representations of Glaukos.

We have established the separate existence of the god, Halios Geron, and have discussed the essential characteristics of the deities who were later identified with him. It remains now to examine the monuments relating to the Old Man of the Sea and the circle of deities associated with him. We shall list these in chronological order as far as practicable.

The famous painted pinax (Fig. 9), found among the late geometric sherds at Praesos in Crete and dating from the seventh century, is our earliest Greek representation which may picture a fish-deity, although some have considered the figure that of a dolphin-rider.[43] It seems improbable, however, that a dolphin-rider is intended, since the bearded figure is distinctly unlike early examples of the youthful dolphin-rider, who is always shown sitting astride his steed. Some have thought that the scene in question represents Theseus borne up to the surface of the

[41] Euripides, *Orestes,* 364 ff. Apoll. Rh., *Argonautika,* I, 1310 ff.

[42] *Brit. Mus. Cat. Coins, Crete and the Aegean Islands* (Wroth), London, 1886, pp. 51-52 and Pls. XII and XIII.

[43] Cf. n. 1 above.

water by a large fish after he received the ring from Amphitrite.[44] Even if we cannot prove that the upper part of the monster was human, the composition certainly resembles that of the Island gem of Fig. 14 (*see* p. 18). It seems likely, therefore, that this is a representation of a hero, possibly Herakles, wrestling with the Old Man of the Sea.

The Argive-Corinthian bronze relief, mentioned in connection with Halios Geron, furnishes definite evidence from the sixth century for the type of Herakles wrestling with Halios Geron (Fig. 10).[45] The relief was found in the Peloponnesos and differs from other reliefs representing the combat of the god with Herakles in that the metamorphoses are suggested by the snake and flame on the head of the monster.

The type of the swimming merman occurs on a bronze matrix from Corfu (Fig. 11).[46] Payne describes the matrix as pure late Protocorinthian work and says it was undoubtedly made in Corinth in the middle of the seventh century. The god has a scaly body joined to the torso under the breasts, large fins and a crescent tail. He appears to be bearded.

Another early representation of the type in question is found on a painted terracotta statuette from Tanagra (Fig. 12).[47] It is one of the so-called "Pappades" figurines, which are rather late, and, in spite of its archaic appearance, might belong to the latter part of the sixth century.[48] It is tempting to connect this figure with the legend of Triton at Tanagra mentioned by Pausanias, but there is no justification for this. The design consists of two mermen antithetically grouped as on many Oriental seal stones.

A number of sea-monsters make their appearance on archaic gems. The so-called Island gems have two types of representations of the man-fish. One, on a gem from Melos, shows the usual bearded merman in the attitude of swimming, but this example is winged (Fig. 13).[49] The second depicts a wingless creature with a scaly fish body in combat with

[44] Elderkin, *op. cit.*, pp. 190-192; Luce, *A.J.A.*, XXVI, 1922, p. 190.

[45] Cf. n. 5 above.

[46] Payne, *Necrocorinthia*, Oxford, 1931, p. 77 and Pl. 45, 3. Also Stuart-Jones, *J.H.S.*, XVI, 1896, p. 330 and Fig. 3 on p. 329 (Ashmolean Museum).

[47] Heuzey, *Les figurines antiques de terre cuite du Musée du Louvre*, Paris, 1883, Pl. XVII, no. 1.

[48] See Ure, *B.S.A.*, XIV, 1908, pp. 309 ff. and by the same author, *Aryballoi and Figurines from Rhitsona*, Cambridge, 1934, pp. 54 ff.

[49] *Ath. Mitt.*, XI, 1886, Pl. VI, no. 10; Furtwängler, *Die Antiken Gemmen*, Berlin and Leipzig, 1900 (hereafter referred to as Furtwängler, *A.G.*), Pl. V, no. 32.

Herakles (Fig. 14).[50] As noted above, the composition of the group is not unlike that found on the Praesos plate and furnishes some evidence for the opinion that the design on the plate represents a hero wrestling with a fish-deity (Fig. 9).

In Sardinia we find a series of late archaic gems depicting sea-monsters. They come from the site of Tharros, a Graeco-Phoenician settlement. The type of the swimming merman is represented. The god usually holds a fish, but occasionally he has a wreath and beaker (Fig. 15b, c, d).[51] The dolphin-rider also appears here and the hippocamp-rider. Although there is some evidence that the Phoenicians carried the worship of a fish-tailed deity to foreign parts, the monsters on these gems are evidently copied from archaic Greek prototypes.

We have proof that Ionic art penetrated as far north as Vettersfelde in Brandenburg. A curious fish of solid gold, decorated with reliefs, was found on this site (Fig. 16).[52] The monument dates from the early fifth century. The upper part of the body is adorned with an "Ionic" frieze; the lower part with a representation of a sea-god leading a school of fishes. The figure has certain features in common with other archaic swimming mermen: the beard, the scaly body and the fish as an attribute. He is, however, distinguished by his long hair which is combed up over his forehead and falls in a curl over his shoulder.

Furtwängler mentions a bronze urn from Capua decorated with a figure of a merman.[53] This was probably made in Cumae at the end of the sixth century.[54]

Corinthian, East Greek, Boeotian and Attic vases offer more examples of the merman type than any other monuments. Hybrid and fantastic monsters of all sorts are common on Corinthian pottery and the man-fish is not lacking. Under what name he was worshipped in Corinth is not known. As stated earlier, some would like to call him Glaukos because Glaukos had associations with Corinth. Because he resembles in type the sea-god found on Attic vases and attested by inscriptions as Triton, Payne called him Triton. Corinthian examples picture the merman apparently "treading-water" or splashing in the surf (Fig. 17).[55]

[50] *Rev. Arch.*, XXVII, 1872, Pl. 12, no. 1; Furtwängler, *A.G.*, Pl. V, no. 30; Walters, *Brit. Mus. Cat. Gems*, no. 212, with full bibliography.

[51] Furtwängler, *A.G.*, Pl. XV, nos. 36, 37 and 38, and Walters, *op. cit.*, nos. 396 and 397.

[52] Furtwängler, "Der Goldfund von Vettersfelde", pp. 25 ff.

[53] *Ibid.*, p. 26, n. 3.

[54] Lamb, *Greek and Roman Bronzes*, London, 1929, pp. 137 ff.

[55] Payne, *op. cit.*, p. 77 and Fig. 22A and B, and nos. 627 and 628 (Wilisch, *Die Altkorinthische Thonindustrie*, Leipzig, 1892, Fig. 41).

These mermen are more playful and amusing than other examples and are not represented nude, but wear a short-sleeved garment. The fish bodies are small and short compared with the long sinuous forms of most archaic mermen. In addition to the representations on vases the merman also occurs on some of the clay plaques from Corinth.[56] On one example he appears in company with Athena, Amphitrite and Poseidon. The second example is unillustrated. Another series of Corinthian vases *may* picture the merman (Fig. 18).[56a] The figures have sickle wings and a long eellike body. This type, which is also clothed, has a decidedly Oriental aspect. It may be a descendant of the old god of vegetation found on Oriental seals (Fig. 19).[56b]

The Ionian or East Greek class of vases provides occasional representations of the swimming merman. On a small vase of Klazomenian fabric the god is pictured with a wreath in his extended hand (Fig. 20).[57] His body is black with a white ventral stripe, the upper part being clothed in a short, white sleeveless jacket dotted with black. On the so-called Northampton amphora, however, which is late Klazomenian under Attic influence, the monster is nude and surrounded by dolphins (Fig. 21), the body is arranged in two large, tense curves and the ventral stripe is ringed like the body of an angle worm.[58] A similar example is seen on another vase of Ionian fabric.[59] Still another typical Ionian example occurs on a fragment of a vase from Naukratis.[60] All of these vases have certain characteristics in common. Quite individual in character and different in type is the figure on an amphora in the Castellani Collection which shows on both sides a man-fish with a complete human torso and genitals, like the archaic type of centaur.[61] This vase is dated between 540 and 520 B.C. The tendency to nudity in the later East Greek examples is perhaps due to Attic influence.

[56] a. *Ant. Denk.*, I, Berlin, 1887, Pl. 7, Fig. 11; Pernice, *Jahr.*, XII, 1897, p. 19, F485 and 765 and Fig. 10. These are all in Berlin.

b. Pernice, *op. cit.*, F654 and 781.

[56a] Payne, *op. cit.*, pp. 76 ff. and Pl. 15, nos. 4 and 5 (Brussels and Syracuse).

[56b] *Illustrated London News*, July 15, 1939, p. 99, third seal, first row. Cf. however, the hybrid monster on the vase from Daphnae in the British Museum, Walters, *History of Ancient Pottery*, London, 1905, I, Fig. 95, p. 351.

[57] *Ant. Denk.*, II, Berlin, 1908, Pl. 56, no. 2.

[58] Gerhard, *op. cit.*, Pls. 317-318; Beazley, *Papers of the British School at Rome*, XI, pp. 1 ff. and Pl. I, 1.

[59] Gerhard, *op. cit.*, Pls. 8-9; Endt, *Beiträge zur Ionische Vasenmalerei*, Prag, 1899, p. 62 and Fig. 43.

[60] Petrie, *Naukratis*, I, London, 1886, Pl. XIII, 9.

[61] Mingazzini, *Vasi della Collezione Castellani, Catalogo*, Rome, 1931, p. 167, no. 409, and Pl. XXXV, 1 and 2.

The so-called Pontic vases, which, in the opinion of Ducati, may have been made in Italy, bear a close relationship to the archaic art of Ionia and Etruria.[62] On one of these vases, in the Bibliothèque Nationale in Paris, part of the decoration consists of a frieze of fantastic animals, among which appears a swimming merman with eellike body (Fig. 22).[63] The figure is nude, the body free from scales as in East Greek examples, the tail small. Most extraordinary in this class are three monsters depicted on the neck of another Pontic vase, now in Rome (Fig. 23).[64] A dolphin's tail is joined to the back of a complete human body, just as the horse's body is joined to the man's back in an archaic centaur.[64a] Some think the artist intended to copy the Assyrian deity with the fish-skin cloak, but more probably this is an invention of the fertile imagination of an Ionian artist.

Examples of the man-fish occur also on a group of vases which may be Boeotian.[65] The first of these is a lekythos, now in the Louvre, on the neck of which the combat of Herakles and Halios Geron (Fig. 24) is represented.[66] The fish body, however, is scaly like those of Attic "Tritons". There is little attempt to represent a struggle; Herakles has merely thrown his arms about the neck of the monster. Of special interest are the protomai of the lion and the snake which appear on the god's body and which symbolize his metamorphoses. This lekythos probably dates in the second quarter of the sixth century. A related vase in Bonn shows Herakles in combat with a fish-god, who is probably Triton, since no metamorphoses are represented.[67] Of provincial workmanship and also from Boeotia is a vase with the single figure of a nude merman carrying a fish in each hand.[67a] A merman, also without Herakles, occurs on a Boeotian kyathos in the Louvre where he is shown as part of

[62] Ducati, *Pontische Vasen*, Berlin, 1932, pp. 1 ff. Cf. Dümmler, *Röm. Mitt.*, II, 1887, pp. 171 ff.

[63] deRidder, *Catalogue des vases peints de la Bibliothèque Nationale*, Paris, 1901-1902, Pl. IV, no. 178; *C.V.A.*, Bibliothèque Nationale, I, Pl. 27, 6 and 28, 7; Ducati, *op. cit.*, Pl. VIIb and XVIa; Sieveking and Hackl, *Die königliche Vasensammlung zu München*, I, Munich, 1912, no. 972, Fig. 183.

[64] Dümmler, *op. cit.*, p. 172, no. 2 and Pl. VIII, 2; Ducati, *op. cit.*, p. 16 and p. 24, Group IV, no. 1.

[64a] Robert, *Archaeologische Hermeneutik*, Berlin, 1919, p. 45, Figs. 30 and 31.

[65] Payne, *op. cit.*, p. 193.

[66] *Rev. Arch.*, 1899, I, p. 8, Fig. 5 (Pottier); *Ath. Mitt.*, XLVII, 1922, p. 56 and p. 60, Fig. 1 (Buschor); Rumpf, *Chalkidische Vasen*, Berlin and Leipzig, 1927, p. 155, G (with full bibliography).

[67] Rumpf, *op. cit.*, p. 155, D (with full bibliography); *Ath. Mitt.*, XLVII, 1922, p. 56, n. 1.

[67a] Langlotz, *Griechische Vasen in Würzburg*, Munich, 1932, no. 464, Pl. 29.

a frieze of fishes.[67b] He is represented as nude and holds in one hand a branch and in the other a fish. Red is used on the face and neck of the monster and his black body is covered with white dots.

The black-figured vases of Attica reveal a preference for compositions depicting the fight between Herakles and the fish-god, although the single figure of a merman is also found. An Attic krater of the early sixth century on which is represented the combat between Herakles and Halios Geron (Fig. 25) shows the hero riding astride the body of the sea-monster and clasping him tightly from behind, as on the Boeotian vase of Fig. 24.[68] The design closely resembles that of the Boeotian vase in other ways: in the clothed figure of the deity and in the metamorphoses suggested by the snake protome on the monster's back and by the snake held in his hand. This vase must be approximately contemporary with the Boeotian lekythos and the bronze plaque from Olympia on which, as we have already seen, the metamorphoses of Halios Geron are represented (Figs. 24 and 10).

On the top of the handle of an aryballos by Nearchos in the Metropolitan Museum of Art two nude "Tritons" are opposed, forming a graceful pattern with their tails.[69] The vase dates about 550 B.C. Somewhat later in time is the delightful Little Master cup, recently discovered at Rhodes, which has on one side the design of a spirited swimming merman and the inscription καλόν: εἶμι ποτήριον (Fig. 26).[70] The figure, although clothed, has a body without scales and more closely resembles Ionian examples than most of the mermen from Attica. A similar clothed merman occurs on another Attic cylix, also recently found at Rhodes[70a] and on a fragment of a Little Master cup discovered on the Acropolis.[71] Additional single figures of "Triton" are found on two vases in the Louvre and on one in Berlin.[72]

The Attic vases of the black-figured style, which belong to the latter

[67b] *B.C.H.*, XXI, 1897-1898, pp. 453, 454 ff. and Fig. 7 on p. 452.

[68] Nicole, *Catalogue des vases peints du Musée National d'Athènes, Suppl.*, Paris, 1911, no. 911; Buschor, *Ath. Mitt.*, XLVII, 1922, p. 56 and Pl. V.

[69] *A.J.A.*, XXXVI, 1932, p. 273, Fig. 2 (Richter).

[70] *Clara Rhodos*, III, 1929, p. 34, no. 3 and Fig. 18.

[70a] *Ibid.*, VIII, p. 71 and Fig. 58.

[71] Graef, *op. cit.*, no. 1575, Pl. 82.

[72] Pottier, *Catalogue des vases antiques de terre cuite du Musée National du Louvre*, Paris, 1899-1906, III, p. 772, F148 (Pottier, *Vases antiques du Louvre*, II, p. 111, Pl. 75); Pottier, *Catalogue des vases antiques, etc.*, 111, p. 813, F397; Furtwängler, *Beschreibung der Vasensammlung im Antiquarium*, Berlin, 1885 (hereafter referred to as *Berlin*), no. 1755. This last example, which is early black-figured, is clothed.

half of the sixth century, for the most part picture the combat between Herakles and the fish-god and show the evolution of the sixth-century type. The god now acquires in inscriptions the definite name of Triton. Fig. 27 is a typical example. Usually a panel on the vase is filled with the wrestling combatants.[72a] Triton is always nude and there is no suggestion of metamorphosis. The two are represented at the height of the struggle with their arms interlocked. Herakles, wearing his lion-skin, conquers the monster in his relentless grip. The pre-Greek sea-god is at last overcome by his northern opponent.

Two poros pediments from the Acropolis present the same combat theme.[73] The better preserved, which belonged to the Old Athena temple on the Acropolis and which probably dates before 550 B.C., shows the body of the monster drawn out in a series of diminishing curves which fill admirably the triangular space of the pediment (Fig. 28). Herakles has thrown his opponent and holds his body firmly on the ground with his own weight. The other half of the pediment was occupied by the famous "Bluebeard", or three-bodied monster with the snaky tail.[74] This monster has been identified with the Old Man of the Sea. Each figure holds in his hand an object which seems to symbolize a metamorphosis. The first is water, the second fire, the third air, typified by a bird. Although the Athenians ordinarily thought of Halios Geron as an old man, probably identical with Nereus, they apparently continued to ascribe to him the power of changing his form. It seems certain that at the time of the pediment, they had already transferred the combat with Herakles to their favorite Triton or to Nereus. The architrave of the temple at Assos treats the combat theme in a fashion similar to what we find on the pediment from the Acropolis.[75]

Additional examples of the merman type occur on the Harpy tomb from Lycia.[76] Here the man-fish is used as a support for the arm of

[72a] Metropolitan Museum, no. 23. 160. 1. *Bulletin of the Metropolitan Museum of Art*, 1925, p. 300.

[73] Dickins, *Catalogue of the Acropolis Museum*, I, Cambridge, 1912, nos. 2, 36; Richter, *The Sculpture and Sculptors of the Greeks*, New Haven, 1929, Fig. 379; Wiegand and others, *Die archaische Poros-Architektur der Akropolis zu Athen*, Cassel and Leipzig, 1904, Pl. IV.

[74] Buschor, "Die Dreileibige", *Ath. Mitt.*, XLVII, 1922, pp. 53 ff., Pl. XV. Cf. Lawrence, *History of Classical Sculpture*, New York and London, 1929, p. 112, Pl. 7b; Richter, *op. cit.*, Fig. 378: Wiegand, *op. cit.*, Pl. IV.

[75] Bacon, *Investigations Assos*, Cambridge (Mass.), 1902-1925, p. 145; Lawrence, *op. cit.*, Pl. 9; Richter, *op. cit.*, Fig. 403.

[76] Pryce, *Catalogue of the Sculpture in the British Museum*, I, pt. 1, London, 1928, p. 125 and Pl. XXIII.

one of the thrones carved in relief on the monument. The pair, which Pausanias tells us formed part of the decoration of the early throne of Apollo Hyakinthos at Amyklai, should be counted among the early Ionic specimens, since they were made by Bathykles of Magnesia.[77] Pausanias is of course using the word in its generic sense.

The only city to use the man-fish as a coin type in the archaic period was Kyzikos.[78] An electrum coin of the late archaic period (*ca.* 480 B.C.) has on its obverse the figure of a merman, nude and bearded (Fig. 59a). The deity reclines on his right arm and holds a wreath in his raised left hand.

We have in Greece, to my knowledge, the name of only one fish-tailed goddess, Eurynome. Pausanias describes her cult statue at an ancient shrine near Phigalia as a ξόανον, the upper part of which had the body of a woman and the lower part that of a fish.[79] This statement is of interest, as the word ξόανον is commonly used to designate primitive statues, usually wooden and of great antiquity, possibly even as old as the Minoan-Mycenaean period.[80] Our extant representations of fish-tailed deities, however, do not seem to be older than the Orientalizing period. As Pausanias' information came from hearsay, since the shrine was open only once a year and he did not see the statue, no definite conclusions can be drawn from the statement. The statue may go back to the very beginnings of Oriental influence, i.e., to about 750 B.C.

Very little is known of Eurynome. Homer describes her as the daughter of Okeanos;[81] Hesiod as the daughter of Okeanos and Tethys, and the mother of the Graces.[82] According to a late author, she was the daughter of Proteus, elsewhere known as Eidothea.[83] Kallimachos mentions a Titaness Eurynome, the mother of the Graces.[84] There was also a tradition that Eurynome had once ruled Olympos with the Titan, Ophion, and that when they were superseded by Kronos and Rhea she jumped into the sea.[85] This act had caused her to be compared with the

[77] Pausanias, III, 18, 9 ff.

[78] *Brit. Mus. Cat. Coins, Mysia, etc.* (Wroth), p. 21, Pl. IV, no. 8.

[79] Pausanias, VIII, 41, 6.

[80] Casson, *The Technique of Early Greek Sculpture*, Oxford, 1933, pp. 50 ff.

[81] *Iliad*, XVIII, 398 ff.

[82] *Theogony*, 358 and 907 ff.

[83] Zenodotos, Schol. on *Odyssey*, IV, 366.

[84] Fr. 471.

[85] Apoll. Rh., I, 503. Cf. Furtwängler, "Bronzefunde aus Olympia", pp. 97 ff. Furtwängler believed that Ophion was of Phoenician origin and the Old Man of the Sea in the Phoenician tradition. He connected Ophion with ὄφις, snake, and held that there is no essential difference between snake- and fish-tailed deities.

Cretan goddesses, Diktynna and Britomartis.[86] The story is that Britomartis, pursued by Minos, jumped into the sea and was caught in a net (δίκτυον) whence she received the name Diktynna.[87] This legend doubtless represents the merging of two virgin goddesses with similar attributes. The ritual leap is interesting because it is associated with other deities, many of whom were connected with the Minoan-Mycenaean age,[88] and because we have seen the same phenomenon in Syria (p. 7). Like Diktynna and Britomartis, Eurynome was identified with Artemis. As Artemis Limnatis she presided over a salt spring near her shrine at Phigalia. It seems probable that her cult at Phigalia was very ancient.

The name Eurynome occurs in other connections. Of special interest is Eurynome, the mother of Bellerophon and the wife of Neptune.[89]

The mermaid was an exceedingly rare type in archaic Greek art. An Attic black-figured vase in the collection of Albert Gallatin in New York City pictures a mermaid pursuing a woman.[90] Two pairs of Tritonesses are represented on a black-figured vase in Munich.[91] They are nude, with the fish-tails starting just below the breasts, as in many archaic mermen. Of the first pair, one holds a net and the other a cup; of the second one plays a flute while the other holds a large cup. A Tritoness, crowned and wearing a mantle, with Dionysos on her back is pictured on both sides of a skyphos in Bonn.[91a] This vase is late black-figured and is dated about 510 B.C. Other archaic examples are seen in Etruscan bronze statuettes from Perugia (Fig. 49).[92]

Besides the ordinary mermaid there are some very unusual female types. A gold ring with ovoid bezel of the type known as "Proto-Ionic" was found recently in the tomb of the Bronze Flavella at Populonia, along with Protocorinthian and Corinthian pottery.[92a] The subject represented is one hitherto unknown: Herakles wrestling with a three-bodied Tritoness. Another curious example occurs on a Corin-

[86] Immerwahr, *Die arkadischen Kulte*, Leipzig, 1891, p. 155.

[87] Kallimachos, *Artem.*, 197. This derivation is a mere play upon words. Diktynna is probably connected with Mt. Dikte in Crete.

[88] Wide, "Theseus und der Meersprung bei Bakchylides", *Festschrift für Otto Benndorf*, Vienna, 1898, pp. 13 ff.

[89] Hyginus, *Fab.*, 157.

[90] *C.V.A.*, Gallatin Collection, III, Ja, Pl. 27, 1 and 5. Heydemann describes a similar vase in the collection of Eugene Piot in Paris, "Pariser Antiken", *Hallische Winckelmannsprogram*, 12, 1887, p. 86, no. 3.

[91] Jahn, *Beschreibung der Vasensammlung König Ludwigs in der Pinakothek zu München*, Munich, 1854, no. 468.

[91a] Greifenhagen, *Arch. Anz.*, 1935, p. 475, no. 38 and Fig. 52.

[92] See p. 33.

[92a] Doro Levi, *Illustrated London News*, Sept. 30, 1933, p. 491.

thian bombylios, recently found at Ialysos in Rhodes. This monster has the head of a woman, the body of a bird with wings and a fish's tail.[92b] A strange monster, which may be female, is carved on a sixth-century ivory relief, also from Ialysos (Fig. 29).[92c] With several similar reliefs, it was apparently intended for the decoration of a wooden box. All were found in an archaic tomb at Ialysos, together with some Attic black-figured pottery. The monster in question is described by Maiuri as a fish-bodied siren. The fishy part includes the entire body up to the neck, the front limbs being somewhat like a seal's flippers. The neck and head are those of a human being with long curling hair. It is difficult to place this type, which is neither purely Greek nor Oriental. The face could be either male or female, since male figures were sometimes beardless on Eastern monuments.

By far the most common type of sea-monster found in Greek lands after the man-fish is the hippocamp or sea-horse. The name hippocamp was used by ancient writers to designate the true sea-horse which inhabits Mediterranean waters. The earliest known reference where the name means a sea-monster is found in Menander.[93] Strabo mentions a statue of Poseidon at Helike in which the god was holding a hippocamp in his hand.[94] Pausanias' expression, *ἵππος εἰκασμένος κήτει τὰ μετὰ τὸ στέρνον* suggests either that the word hippocamp was not familiar to him or else that he feared it might not be understood by his readers.[95]

The origin of the hippocamp type is more difficult to establish than the origin of the merman, as there is thus far no evidence of the occurrence of the type in Oriental art. There are some examples of hippocamps on a Cretan prism seal of Minoan times (Fig. 30), but they are nothing like the archaic Greek hippocamps and seem rather to be representations of real sea-horses.[96] A curved tail with small fins is attached to a horse's head. Again, seven gold ornaments in the form of hippocamps were found in the third grave at Mycenae (Fig. 31).[97] With their heads turned back and tails curled upward, they have little in

[92b] Maiuri, *Clara Rhodos*, III, p. 59, Tomb 33, no. 12 and Pl. VII.

[92c] Maiuri, Annuario, VI-VII, pp. 322 ff. and Fig. 216A.

[93] Laevius, Frm. 21.

[94] Strabo, VIII, 7, 2.

[95] Pausanias, II, 1, 9.

[96] Evans, *J.H.S.*, XVII, 1897, p. 335 and Fig. 4b (Copenhagen).

[97] Schliemann, *Mycenae*, New York, 1880, p. 184 and Fig. 280. Perrot and Chipiez, *Histoire de l'art dans l'antiquité*, VI, Paris, 1894, p. 834 and Fig. 419. Cf. Bosanquet, *J.H.S.*, XXIV, 1904, p. 323, no. 4902. Sea-horses from a tomb at Mycenae (Fig. 1c) resemble Mediterranean sea-horses. The fin is amplified into a sort of butterfly wing.

common with early Greek hippocamps. Some scholars, nevertheless, have tried to see a connection. Evidences of Oriental contact at Mycenae make it barely possible that the two may have had a common ancestor in the Orient.

The significance of the hippocamp is an equally difficult problem, since he plays no part in any mythological tale. Some have thought that the horse was symbolic of the waves of the sea. Poseidon riding a hippocamp or Poseidon in a chariot drawn by hippocamps would then represent Poseidon borne by the waves. Another idea is that the monster is intended as a likeness of a real sea-horse, but our knowledge of sea-horses does not justify this theory. Probably the hippocamp is a purely fantastic monster, which served sometimes as a symbol of the sea. Often the animal seems merely to be used for decorative purposes.

Island gems furnish the earliest representations of the hippocamp aside from possible examples from Crete and Mycenae. There are three types represented on Island gems. One with a long, prehensile finless tail (Fig. 32) might be derived from the sea-horse, but for the wings and horse's legs which indicate a hybrid animal.[98] This hippocamp has a peculiar head-gear which some have taken for horns, but it is generally agreed that this is merely an external decoration. A second type, also winged, has a long curved tail (Fig. 33) which, however, ends in a crescentlike formation, suggesting a fish- or a dolphin-tail.[99] In both of these monsters the horse's head and legs are joined directly to the body of the sea-serpent or fish. Still a third type resembles a winged horse as far as the hips, where a fish-tail takes the place of hind legs (Fig. 34).[100]

The hippocamp is represented on a few Graeco-Phoenician gems from Sardinia. Once it is shown with a youthful rider who holds a trident in his right hand and guides a steed with his left (Fig. 15a).[101] The tail of the monster stands up behind. On another gem a winged hippocamp is pictured without a rider.[102] Although some of these gems are decidedly archaic in style, Furtwängler dates none of them before 500 B.C.

A bronze urn found at Capua is decorated with an animal frieze

[98] Ross, *Reisen auf den griechischen Inseln des ägäischen Meeres*, Stuttgart and Tübingen, 1840-1852, III, p. 21.

[99] Furtwängler, *A.G.*, Pl. V, no. 21; Perrot and Chipiez, *op. cit.*, VI, p. 851, Fig. 432, no. 13; *J.H.S.*, XVII, 1897, Pl. III, no. 13; Walters, *Brit. Mus. Cat. Gems*, no. 210, Pl. VII. Cf. also Walters, no. 170.

[100] *Ath. Mitt*, 1886, Pl. VI, no. 19.

[101] Furtwängler, *A.G.*, Pl. XV, no. 35.

[102] Walters, *op. cit.*, Pl. VII, no. 398.

which includes two hippocamps.[103] The tails are pointing downward as in Ionic and Etruscan examples of the monster. The urn was probably made at Cumae about 500 B.C.

East Greek and Corinthian vases do not furnish as many examples of the hippocamp as of the merman. There is, however, in Goluchow a Corinthian krater which has around its mouth an animal frieze with two hippocamps of Ionic type.[104] The hippocamp is also represented on a fragment of a Laconian cup in Leipzig.[105] An Ionic-Etruscan amphora in the Villa Giulia has a figure of a hippocamp on each side of the shoulder.[106] These examples are all wingless. On a fragment from Daphnae, however, the monster is represented with wings.[107]

Like the man-fish the hippocamp is sometimes represented on the animal friezes of Pontic vases (Fig. 35).[108] He is wingless and riderless. The horse body is well developed, with a small belly fin at the point of transition. The fish body forms a single curve with the tail pointing downward. The animals appear to be swimming.

The hippocamp was not common in Attica in the archaic period. On several Attic black-figured vases, however, an old man, perhaps a variant of Halios Geron, is represented riding a hippocamp (Fig. 36). This animal, like almost all hippocamps except those depicted on Island gems, has the forepart of a horse's body as well as the head and fore-legs. He appears to be galloping. The fishy part is scaly like that of "Triton" on black-figured vases. The monster may be winged or not. The rider, who carries a trident, is usually called Nereus, but the attribution cannot be certain.[109] Other designs with the hippocamp are rare on Attic black-figured vases. There is, however, in Athens a lekythos which shows a bearded man and two women, one of whom grasps the tail of a hippocamp.[110]

The only archaic coins with representations of hippocamps have come from Magna Graecia and Sicily. A hippocamp with sickle wings is used as a reverse type on Tarentine coins of about 500 B.C. (Fig.

[103] *Mon. dell'Inst.*, XI, Pl. VI, no. 3. Cf. n. 54 above.

[104] *C.V.A.*, Goluchow, Musée Czartoryski, Pl. 7, 1 c-d.

[105] *Arch. Anz.*, XXXVIII-IX, 1923-24, p. 82, Fig. 19; *J.H.S.*, 1932, p. 26, Fig. 2.

[106] *C.V.A.*, Villa Giulia, III, IV, Bn, Pl. 2.

[107] Petrie, *Tanis*, II, 1888, Pl. XXXI, 11.

[108] Ducati, *op. cit.*, p. 12 and Pls. V-VI, XVIa. Sieveking and Hackl, *op. cit.*, Figs. 104, 183. Fig. 35 is in Würzburg.

[109] Overbeck, *Kunstmythologie*, Leipzig, 1871-1889, s.v. "Poseidon" pp. 217 ff. For complete list of vases see *Appendix*, pp. 97-98.

[110] Nicole, *op. cit.*, no. 932.

37a).[111] The tail is lowered and the legs are posed as those of hippocamps on Pontic vases.

Another important sea-monster represented in Greek art is the marine dragon who is known both by his Latin name *pistrix* and his Greek name κῆτος. The word κῆτος is used by Homer to mean any large fish or sea-monster. Once, however, Homer uses the term when he is apparently referring to the story of Hesione and her rescue by Herakles.[112] On a Corinthian vase depicting the story of Perseus and Andromeda the monster is labeled κῆτος (Fig. 38).[113] Unfortunately only the head is represented, with long snout, open jaws and protruding tongue.

The most prevalent theory in regard to the origin of the marine dragon or *ketos* is that it is derived from the little sea-horse.[114] The chief reason for this belief seems to be the spiked mane which is characteristic of so many specimens. In some cases, however, such a derivation seems out of the question. A Minoan clay seal impression shows a boatman having an encounter with a sea-monster of which only the head is preserved (Fig. 39).[115] This creature with its open canine jaws and large erect ears bears a striking resemblance to some of the *kete* represented on Hellenic monuments. Surely we have here the ancestor of the Greek monster. It is possible that we have a similar example on a Mycenaean wall painting.[116] Some of the *kete* represented on archaic Greek monuments are without the spiked mane of which certain authorities seem inclined to make so much. The Minoans and Mycenaeans might well have had a legend of a doglike sea-monster.[117] The legend of Andromeda has been brought forward as an argument for the Oriental origin of the *ketos*, on the theory that the legend was at first not attached to Perseus, but came from Syria, where it was connected with human sacrifice and the worship of some fish-formed deity.[118] Other scholars, however, consider the Andromeda episode purely Greek.

[111] *Brit. Mus. Cat. Coins, Italy* (Poole), pp. 166-167; I.-B. and K, Pl. XI, 34; Evans, "The Horseman of Tarentum", *Numismatic Chronicle*, 1889, Pl. I, 4.

[112] *Iliad*, XX, 144 ff.

[113] *Mon. dell'Inst.*, X, Pl. 52.

[114] Furtwängler, "Goldfund von Vettersfelds", p. 28.

[115] Evans, *B.S.A.*, IX, 1902-1903, p. 57 and Fig. 36; *Ath. Mitt.*, XXXI, 1906, p. 50, Fig. 1. This is now in the museum in Candia, Crete.

[116] Studniczka, *Ath. Mitt.*, XXXI, 1906, p. 51 and Fig. 2; *Eph. Arch.*, 1887, Pl. 11, left above, p. 168.

[117] Cf. Marinatos, 'Αρχ. Δελ., 1926, pp. 57 ff. Marinatos believes that the *ketos* had as its prototype a ferocious fish, the Καρχαρίας.

[118] Pauly-Wissowa, s.v. "Andromeda" Vs. this view Roscher's *Lexikon*, s.v.

Probably the oldest Hellenic representation of the *ketos* is to be found on a gem from Epidaurus Limera dated about 700 B.C.[119] The monster here pictured swims beneath a galley (Fig. 40). He has the characteristic canine head with open jaws and large erect ears. Other prominent features are the large fins, the scaly serpentlike body and the fishtail. Another example, nearly as old, has recently been discovered at Dreros in Crete.[119a] A bronze Gorgoneion, which belongs in the first decade of the sixth century, has two beautiful *kete* engraved antithetically on the forehead.

Additional examples of early date with representations of the *ketos* are found on vases. A vase from Southern Italy of imitation Corinthian ware, shows a figure of a sea-monster with the body of a fish and the head of a dog or wolf.[120] Another vase of uncertain fabric pictures a sea-monster of somewhat similar type devouring a man.[121]

Some sea-monsters, usually classed with the *ketos*, are painted on clay pinakes from Corinth. There is always a rider on the tablets, who is probably either Melikertes or Poseidon. The best preserved specimen is a highly fantastic monster whose head with the horns and beard bears a striking resemblance to a goat (Fig. 41).[122] The long neck and the body, as far as it is preserved, are covered with scales. The rider carries a trident and what appears to be a mussel shell. On another plaque the monster somewhat resembles a seal[123] with whiskers although most of the head is missing. A third example is too poorly preserved to characterize.[124] The body has no scales and is partly covered with red dots.

Coins of Catana beginning at the end of the sixth century have the design of a pistrix swimming beneath the feet of the river-god, Acheloos.[125] Although the large head and spiky crest suggest the sea-horse, it seems improbable that there is any connection even in this case, since the pistrix has a beard, large ears and an open denticulated jaw.

Compared with the hippocamp and merman the *ketos* was a rare

"Perseus" and Halliday, *Indo-European Folk-Tales and Greek Legend*, Cambridge, 1933, pp. 121ff.

[119] Furtwängler, *A.G.*, Pl. VI, 34 (Collection of Sir Arthur Evans).

[119a] *Arch. Anz.*, 1936, p. 219, Fig. 4. Cf. the coins of Itanos, Fig. 58b.

[120] Pottier, *Vases antiques du Louvre*, I, E421 and Pl. 40; Marinatos, *op. cit.*, pp. 58 ff. and Fig. 3, 3.

[121] Rumpf, *op. cit.*, p. 155, F; Marinatos, *op. cit.*, p. 59, Fig. 3, 2.

[122] *Ant. Denk.*, I, Pl. 7, 26.

[123] *Ibid.*, II, Pl. 39, 8.

[124] *Ibid.*, II, Pl. 39, 16a.

[125] I.-B. and K., Pl. XIII, no. 18.

type in archaic Greek art. It is of interest to find all three types of sea-monsters as well as the story of Andromeda represented on early Corinthian monuments.

We thus see that Greece made extensive use of the man-fish in the archaic period. Several types were employed. Aside from the swimming merman, who was represented as clothed on East Greek monuments as a rule, and nude in Attica, although exceptions occur, the favorite type represented Herakles wrestling with a man-fish. Corinth offered an individual type in its "water-treading" and "water-splashing" examples, and the East Greek class the extraordinary type of the dolphin-man.

The mermaid was little used. The hippocamp played an important rôle, especially on Island and Graeco-Phoenician gems, on coins of Magna Graecia and Sicily, on East Greek and black-figured vases. The hippocamp rider appears to be the only type developed aside from the usual swimming examples, both winged and wingless. The type with the tail attached to a horse's body is unusual. The *ketos* or marine dragon, probably derived from a Minoan prototype, is commonest in harbor towns and seems to be a favorite sea-monster at Corinth. The individualized variants of the different types occur in the East Greek and Corinthian examples.

In conclusion, it is interesting to note that an example of a sea-monster on an Egyptian coffin of the Twenty-sixth Dynasty shows well the influence of archaic Greek art on contemporary Egypt.[126] The coffin, which is of unknown provenance, is now in the Museum of the City of Gloucester, England. It is in human form, and the inconveniently curved space below the necklace on each side is filled, as in some archaic Greek pediments, with the tail of a sea-monster. To the tail is attached a horse's head in a manner which suggests a little the designs on Island gems. Although some features of this hippocamp are Egyptian, the idea for such a monster must surely have been borrowed from the Greeks.

[126] *British School of Archaeology in Egypt, Studies*, II, *Historical Studies*, London, 1911, pp. 39 ff., Pl. XXI (Murray). Mlle. M. Werbrouck of the Brussels Museum most kindly called my attention to this coffin.

III

SEA-MONSTERS IN ARCHAIC ETRUSCAN ART

The Etruscans were very fond of representing fish-tailed monsters, especially on their grave monuments.[1] Apparently they imagined the next world to be inhabited by various demons which included creatures with fish-tails. Unlike the Greeks the Etruscans had many types of sea-monsters, some of which represented a mixture of Greek with native Etruscan elements. The results were often quite extraordinary. Many Etruscan examples, however, follow fairly closely their Greek prototypes.

The hippocamp and merman are the favorite types found on Etruscan monuments in the archaic period. On the stamped vases of red ware from Caere, swimming mermen are represented in friezes along with men and animals, much as they appear on Pontic vases.[2] They are nude and bearded and swim with arms extended. The same type occurs also on a bronze disc from Perugia.[3] Two mermen swimming toward each other are carved in relief on an Etruscan cinerary urn of the archaic period.[4]

Other interesting examples closely resemble Greek conceptions, for instance the archaic statuette in the Boston Museum (Fig. 42)[5] and a primitive statuette of a bearded merman in the British Museum.[6] Some, on the other hand, present more individual characteristics, *e.g.*, the nude merman on a bronze ornament in the Metropolitan Museum (Fig. 43).[7] This vigorous, pudgy little figure has two scaly fish-tails on which he leans with both hands. The type with two tails is almost unknown in archaic

[1] Waser, *Skylla und Charybdis in der Literatur und Kunst der Griechen*, Zurich, 1894, pp. 87 ff. Cf. R. Hennig, *Zur Entstehung der Charybdis- und Skylla-Fabel*, Stuttgart, 1931.

[2] See *Appendix*, p. 97.

[3] Micali, *Monumenti per servire alla storia degli Antichi Popoli Italiani*, Florence, 1833, Pl. XXXI, 4.

[4] Rumpf, *Katalog der Etruskischen Skulpturen* (*Staatliche Museen zu Berlin, Katalog der Sammlung antiker Skulpturen*, I), Berlin, 1928, E15 and Pl. 11.

[5] 01.7508.

[6] Walters, *Catalogue of the Bronzes in the Department of Greek and Roman Antiquities in the British Museum* (hereafter referred to as *Brit. Mus. Cat. Bronzes*), London, 1899, no. 485.

[7] Richter, *Greek, Etruscan and Roman Bronzes in the Metropolitan Museum of Art*, New York, 1915, pp. 31 ff., no. 49.

art though examples are seen on several antefixes in the Villa Giulia (Fig. 44),[8] where the deity is of the so-called "Typhon" type with entwined serpents joined to the human body in place of legs. Fins on the shoulder, however, make it clear that we are dealing with a marine deity. Equally individualized is the merman on an archaic ivory relief of the sixth century from Corneto (Fig. 45).[9] A nude sea-monster with Semitic hooked nose and a fish in either hand reclines on cushions on the floor of the sea. The resemblance of this figure to certain examples on Cypriote monuments has been pointed out.[10] The relief may have have been made by an East Greek artist, but the inorganic quality of the anatomy and the treatment of the hair point to Etruscan workmanship. A most curious specimen of a merman with a boy rider is probably late archaic.[11] Three bearded heads with three busts are symmetrically grouped about a pisciform bronze handle. All of the figures discussed are nude.

Quite in contrast to these nude mermen is the clothed specimen on one of the famous bronze reliefs from Perugia (Fig. 46).[11a] The relief once decorated the box of a chariot. Hunting scenes are combined here in an unusual fashion with sea-monsters—the hippocamp and merman. This merman is one of the most extraordinary in ancient art. The figure is long-haired and bearded and is clothed in a close-fitting garment. It becomes a sea-monster solely by virtue of the fins on the garment. The figure has a thoroughly Oriental look. The clothed man-fish would seem to be more at home in the Orient, as the man in the fish-skin cloak on Oriental monuments indicates.

[8] Della Seta, *Museo di Villa Giulia*, I, Rome, 1918, pp. 261 ff., no. 10232. For examples of this type without fins in archaic Etruscan art, cf. Sieveking, *Die Bronzen der Sammlung Loeb*, Munich, 1913, p. 21, Pl. 9; Richter, *op. cit.*, no. 482. An antefix from Capua, Walters, *Catalogue of the Terracottas in the British Museum*, London, 1903 (hereafter referred to as to as *Brit. Mus. Cat. Terracottas*) B 587 is very similar.

[9] *Mon. dell'Inst.*, VI-VII, Pl. 46 and *Annali*, 1860, p. 478; *Röm. Mitt.*, XXII, 1906, pp. 322 ff., Pl. XVI; Ducati, *Storia dell'Arte Etrusca*, Florence, 1927, Pl. 126, Fig. 330, 2.

[10] Pollak, *Röm. Mitt.*, XXII, 1906, pp. 322 ff.

[11] Babelon-Blanchet, *Catalogue des bronzes antiques de la Bibliothèque Nationale*, Paris, 1895, no. 65; Reinach, *Repertoire de la Statuaire grecque et romaine*, 2nd ed., Paris, 1906-1924 (hereafter referred to as Reinach, *Stat.*) II, p. 413, no. 3.

[11a] Micali, *op. cit.*, Pl. XXVIII; *Röm. Mitt.*, IX, 1894, pp. 256 ff. and Fig. 1; *Ant. Denk.*, II, Pl. 15; Brunn-Bruckmann, *Denkmäler griechischer und römischer Skulptur*, Munich, 1888-date, Pls. 586-587; Furtwängler, *Kleine Schriften*, Munich, 1912, II, pp. 331 and Pls. 33-34; Ducati, *op. cit.*, Pl. 107, Figs. 284-285; Lamb, *op. cit.*, p. 123, Pl. 49c. These reliefs are in Munich.

Other examples of the clothed man-fish occur on an archaic bronze handle, now in the British Museum (Fig. 47).[12] At each end is a merman *de face*. Their foreheads are bald; they have long beards and moustaches and long hair falling down their backs. They wear short girt chitons with apoptygma. Walters includes the piece among archaic Etruscan bronzes. The neatness and precision are worthy of archaic Greek work. Another handle, almost identical with this, is in the National Museum at Naples.[13]

The swimming man-fish was occasionally used by the Etruscans as a decoration for the gable spaces on their tombs (Fig. 48a). The tapering tail made a convenient filling ornament, though the designs probably had a much profounder meaning to the Etruscan, doubtless symbolizing the soul's journey to the West. On one gable of the Tomba del Mare, there is an antithetical composition with a merman and a hippocamp on either side (Fig. 48a).[14] The arms of the merman are outstretched as if he were swimming vigorously.

We have already noted the fact that Etruscan bronze statuettes give us some of our finest examples of the mermaid.[15] On the bronze in the Bibliothèque Nationale illustrated in Fig. 49, the nude upper body is erect and supported by the arms with the palms of the hands downward. She has a scaly fish body with small fins in various places.

A monster which is certainly a fish-bodied siren is found occasionally on Etruscan monuments. One of the bronzes from Perugia furnishes the best example. A woman's head and bird's feet are attached to a body with scales, fins and a fish-tail—all highly conventionalized but quite unmistakable (Fig. 50).[16] The same monster seems to be represented on a bronze from Catania, which is probably also Etruscan.[17] The upper body is covered with a short cloak, below which are the legs of a bird. There is probably a third representation of the type on an Etruscan vase in Munich.[18] This monster is probably also symbolic.

It is a striking fact that the hippocamp, though little used in archaic Greek art, appears frequently on Etruscan monuments. While most

[12] Six, *J.H.S.*, VI, 1885, p. 284 and Pl. D; *Brit. Mus. Cat. Bronzes*, no. 576.

[13] Ruesch, *Guida Illustrata del Museo Nazionale di Napoli*, Naples, 1911, no. 1529, Fig. 83; Reinach, *Stat.*, III, p. 249, no. 1.

[14] Weege, *Etruskische Malerei*, Halle, 1921, p. 87, Fig. 75.

[15] Petersen, *Röm. Mitt.*, IX, 1894, p. 303, nos. 28-31; Micali, *op. cit.*, Pl. XXIX, 5; *Mon. dell'Inst.*, I, Pl. XVIII; Babelon-Blanchet, *op. cit.*, no. 66; Reinach, *Stat.*, II, p. 413, no. 2.

[16] *Röm. Mitt.*, IX, 1894, p. 305, Fig. 10.

[17] Petersen, *Röm. Mitt.*, XII, 1897, p. 116, Fig. 2.

[18] Sieveking and Hackl, *op. cit.*, no. 871 and Fig. 130.

early Greek hippocamps are winged, the Etruscans show a decided preference for the wingless type. There are, however, a few exceptions, such as the conventionalized ones with stiff wings on the cult stairway from Tarquinia (Fig. 51).[19] The riderless type such as we commonly find in Etruscan animal friezes prevails on all classes of Etruscan monuments, though there are one or two examples with riders (cf. Fig. 52). In this period the monster seems to be used for the most part in a decorative way, but the representations are probably symbolic.

New marine types arise in Etruscan art such as the monster on two Etruscan black-figured vases with the head and forepaws of a lion and the tail of a fish.[20] The sea-dog is also used to decorate the tomb gable (Fig. 48b).[21] The conservatism of the Greeks in the invention of new marine types is striking when compared with that of the Etruscans. The Greeks in the archaic period confined themselves for the most part to three established types, the merman, the hippocamp and the *ketos*, with occasional use of the mermaid. The Etruscan artist, on the other hand, seems to have invented more freely. This is readily seen in the individualized mermen of Figs. 44 and 45 and in wholly new types such as the siren-fish, the sea-dog and the lion-fish.

Among the earliest examples of hippocamps are those on the red clay stamped ceramics from Caere, which are dated about the middle of the sixth century. Here, as in the case of the merman, the monster forms part of an animal frieze.[22] Similar examples appear on the animal friezes on *bucchero* and black-figured vases.[23] A single hippocamp with scales in white is found on a black-figured vase, imitating Attic ware.[24] The hippocamp also appears in animal friezes on the bronze disc from Perugia and on the Perugia chariot reliefs, where in one case it merely serves as filling ornament (Fig. 46).[25] Bronze braziers with figures of hippocamps at each of the four corners show that the original character of the animal had been forgotten and that they came to be more purely decorative, though perhaps as a part of Etruscan tomb furniture they were

[19] Mühlestein, *Die Kunst der Etrusker, Die Ursprünge*, Berlin, 1929, Figs. 206-207.

[20] Moses, *Vases of Sir H. Englefield*, London, 1848, Pl. 29; *Brit. Mus. Cat. Vases*, II, B 68. Cf. Etruscan coin, I.-B. and K., Pl. XII, 33.

[21] Weege, *op. cit.*, Beilage III, Fig. 4; *Ant. Denk.*, II, Hülfstafel 41, Fig. 4.

[22] See *Appendix* p. 98.

[23] Micali, *op. cit.*, Pl. XXVI, no. 3 (*bucchero*); Sieveking and Hackl, *op. cit.*, no. 938, Fig. 172 (black-figured).

[24] *Brit. Mus. Cat. Vases*, II, B 68. Cf. n. 20 above.

[25] See n. 3 and n. 11a above.

intended to suggest the journey or passage to the other world.[26] Bronze statuettes of hippocamps have also been found, two at Perugia.[27]

Hippocamps, often in antithetical composition, formed a favorite motive in the painted gables of Etruscan tombs. Examples are found in the Tomba dei Tori, the Tomba del Mare, the Tomba dei Vasi Dipinti and the Tomba del Barone (Figs. 48a, b and c).[28] The body is drawn out in a shallow curve to fit the long, narrow triangle. Still another example in painting is found on an archaic tufa sarcophagus from Civita Castellana where two hippocamps are pictured on the cover, each grasping a flower with tendrils.[29] Other examples of the wingless type are found on Etruscan rings.[30]

A possible example of an Etruscan hippocamp in sculpture is seen in Fig. 52, although a figure of "Triton" may be intended.[31]

[26] *Brit. Mus. Cat. Bronzes*, nos. 385, 387 and 388; Schumacher, *Beschreibung der Sammlung antiker Bronzen in Karlsruhe*, Karlsruhe, 1891, no. 382; deRidder, *Bronzes antiques du Louvre*, Paris, 1913-1915, I, no. 208, Pl. 21 (Reinach, *Stat.*, II, 2, p. 700, no. 1).

[27] Babelon-Blanchet, *op. cit.*, no. 794; Reinach, *Stat.*, II, 2, p. 699, no. 4; *Röm. Mitt.*, IX, 1894, p. 303. nos. 32-33 and Fig. 2 (p. 271).

[28] Weege, *op. cit.*, Figs. 55 and 75 and Beilage III, 1, 2 and 4; Ducati, *op. cit.*, Pl. 79, Fig. 229.

[29] *Arch. Anz.*, 1903, pp. 38 ff. (Berlin).

[30] Furtwängler, *A.G.*, Pl. VI, nos. 27-28, and Pl. LXV, no. 2. Furtwängler (*A.G.*, III, p. 83) calls these Ionic under Egyptian influence, but I follow Ducati (*Pontische Vasen*, p. 12) who calls them Etruscan.

[31] Karo, *Die Antike*, I, p. 234 and Fig. 13; Mühlestein, *op. cit.*, Fig. 226. This piece is in the Villa Guilia.

IV

GREEK MONUMENTS OF THE FIFTH CENTURY WITH REPRESENTATIONS OF SEA-MONSTERS

The popularity of sea-monsters had so waned by the close of the sixth century that few examples are found on red-figured vases or indeed on any monuments of the fifth century. Artists were more inclined to use these figures merely for auxiliary or purely decorative purposes. Hybrid forms and monsters had less of an appeal for the Greek of the fifth century than for his forebears of the Orientalizing period or even for the Greeks of the sixth century who were more closely in contact with the East. We shall see that the leading centers which made extensive use of sea-monsters in this period were Southern Italy, the islands, especially Melos and Crete, and Etruria. Striking also is the humanization of the earlier monstrous figures.

The merman type seldom occurs on large monuments of the fifth century. The only examples known to me are found on two sculptured groups from a fifth-century temple at Locri, built in 493 B.C. They represent the Dioscuri on horseback crossing a river, which is personified in each case by a figure of a merman supporting the body of a horse. These mermen are bearded and have fan-shaped tails. Like many fifth-century examples, they wear short chitons (Fig. 53).[1]

The earliest red-figured vases, dating from the sixth century, sometimes repeated the black-figured motifs. A well-known red-figured stamnos in the British Museum, signed by the potter Pamphaios and attributed to the painter Oltos, shows Herakles in combat with the river-god Acheloos, here depicted as a man-fish resembling the black-figured Triton (Fig. 54).[2] The type is an adaptation of earlier designs depicting the combat of Herakles with Triton. The actual contest of Herakles and Triton was represented on a red-figured cylix, which has unfortunately been lost (Fig. 55).[3] The composition differs from black-figured specimens in that Herakles, the contest over, rests triumphantly in one of the curves of Triton's body, while three Nereids hurry to Nereus with the news. The combat scene also appears on a gem of the severe

[1] *Arch. Anz.*, 1927, p. 413 and Ferri, *Boll. d'Arte*, Sept., 1927, p. 167 and p. 159, Fig. 1. The groups are now in Naples.

[2] *Brit. Mus. Cat. Vases*, III, E 437; *C.V.A.*, Brit. Mus. V, Group III Ic, Pl. 19, 1b.

[3] Published in *Annali*, 1882, Pl. K.

style, but here Herakles, victorious, holds his victim by the throat (Fig. 56).[4] After this time the motif of Herakles and Triton disappears and new functions for Triton come to the fore. No longer a dreadful monster to be overcome by the greatest of heroes, he becomes a humble aide in the household of his parents, Poseidon and Amphitrite, and the friend and playmate of the Nereids.

Examples of the merman type on red-figured vases, except at the very beginning, show the monster clothed in a short chiton which completely covers the joining of the fish and human bodies. The fish body is scaly and curved in a manner characteristic of the archaic Tritons. The usual attributes are a staff and a dolphin or some other fish. In two instances, the deity is labeled "Triton."

A small amphora by the Berlin Painter, now in the Fogg Museum at Harvard, shows the changing conception in the merman type of the fifth century.[5] The deity, probably Triton, is clad in a chiton and himation which completely cover the joining of the human and fish parts of the body. The god wears a wreath on his head and carries a staff in one hand and a fish in the other. A similar figure, also with a fish in its hand, is represented on a red-figured bowl in Berlin,[6] while the same clothed figure holding a trident is pictured on two red-figured cylices of late style, one of which is in the British Museum, the other in the Laborde Collection in Paris.[7]

This type also occurs occasionally on vases in connection with Peleus and Thetis and the Nereids. We find a similar clothed figure, labeled "Triton," in company with Nereus and the Nereids on a red-figured cylix, attributed to the Kleophrades Painter.[8] The fish part is entirely destroyed except for a few scales which emerge below his short chiton. Nereus, also designated by an inscription, is an old man seated on a throne. Each holds a staff in one hand and a fish in the other. On another vase in Naples, on which is pictured the struggle of Peleus and Thetis, a Nereid is shown hastening toward a bearded "Triton," who is dressed in a chiton and wears a wreath on his head.[9]

[4] *Brit. Mus. Cat. Gems*, no. 474 and Pl. VIII; Furtwängler, *A.G.*, Pl. IX, no. 2.

[5] Beazley, *Attic Red-figured Vases in American Museums*, Cambridge (Mass.), 1918, p. 39, Fig. 22.

[6] *Berlin* 2608.

[7] a. *Brit. Mus. Cat. Vases*, III, E 109; Lenormant-deWitte, *op. cit.*, III, Pl. 33. b. Lenormant-deWitte, *op. cit.*, Pl. 34.

[8] *Brit. Mus. Cat. Vases*, III, E 73; P. Gardner, *Journal of Philology*, VII, pp. 215 ff. Pl. A. Beazley, *J.H.S.*, XIX, 1910, pp. 63 ff., no. 32.

[9] Heydemann, *Die Vasensammlung des Museo Nazionale zu Neapel*, Berlin, 1872 (hereafter referred to as *Naples*), no. 2638; *Mon. dell'Inst.*, I, 37.

New in the fifth century, apparently, is the design in which Triton supports Theseus or carries him in his arms.[9a] The finest example is found on the beautiful cylix in the Louvre by the Panaitios Painter.[10] The merman, whom an inscription gives us the right to call Triton, supports the youthful Theseus as he receives a wreath from his mother, Amphitrite. He is nude and the joining of the scaly body to the human head and shoulders is clearly visible. Like earlier examples, he is bearded.

Theseus' adventure is again treated on the Bologna krater by a late fifth-century vase painter, known as the Kadmos Painter.[11] The hero is held in the arms of Triton as he receives his mother's gift. This Triton is elaborately dressed in a long chiton, beneath which extends his disproportionately large tail tied in a knot. His head is adorned with a wreath. The spiked fin of the tail is typical of fifth-century mermen. It has been suggested that this vase may echo a painting in the Theseum at Athens which Pausanius attributed to Mikon.[12]

We find the same type on one of the so-called Melian reliefs (Fig. 57).[13] A merman, probably Triton, is represented carrying a youth. His fish body is twice curved and has a toothed dorsal fin and a smaller belly fin. The tail is crescent-shaped. The human part which extends from the glutaeus upward is nude. The god has long hair and a pointed beard. Waves and a dolphin beneath Triton's body indicate the setting. This piece belongs to the early group of Melian reliefs, which began in the late seventies of the fifth century and extended into the sixties.

A painted marble vase in the Walters Gallery in Baltimore which will be discussed more fully below (*see* p. 40), has a representation of a nude "Triton" in front of a chariot drawn by a pair of hippocamps (Fig. 62). He is youthful and beardless and in this respect differs from the mermen ordinarily represented on fifth-century monuments. Youthful "Tritons" were common enough in the Hellenistic age. Further, the design of this vase is of particular interest in view of the fact that it appears to be otherwise unknown before the Hellenistic period.[13a]

[9a] Triton bearing Theseus would be a revival of a seventh-century motif if the pinax from Crete is thus interpreted. Cf. p. 10 n. 1.

[10] Furtwängler-Reichhold, *Griechische Vasenmalerei*, Munich, 1900-date, I, p. 27 and Pl. V. Pottier, *Vases antiques*, Pl. 104, G 104.

[11] *Mon. dell'Inst.*, Suppl., Pl. 21.

[12] Pausanias, I, 17, 2.

[13] Jacobsthal, *Die melische Reliefs*, Berlin-Wilmersdorf, 1931, p. 17, no. 3 and Pl. 3.

[13a] Cf. *Arch. Anz.*, 1925, pp. 34 ff. and Fig. 1. Poseidon is represented on a Hellenistic cup riding in a chariot drawn by hippocamps. In front swims a young

There seems to be no doubt, however, that the monument belongs to the fifth century.

On fifth-century coins the merman is nude and ordinarily has the toothed or spiked fin. Several cities used this monster as a coin type, particularly Itanos in Crete (Fig. 58a and b and Fig. 59c).[14] The name of the deity represented here is unknown, but, as tradition makes Itanos a Phoenician settlement, it is possible that the god was Phoenician. Those who believe Glaukos was at home in Crete wish to call him Glaukos. The deity is shown with a complete human torso entirely nude. The fish body, which takes the place of legs, curves up behind and ends in a crescent-shaped tail. The god is pictured with a fish in his left hand, striking downward with a trident which he holds in his right. This type, with minor variations, continued from about 480 to 450 B.C. Late in the fifth century we find a similar deity on coins of Campanian Cumae (Fig. 59b),[15] and such a type was then in use at Akragas in Sicily and Karystos in Euboea.[16] Contemporary with these are the coins of Arados with the man-fish as an obverse type (Fig. 59f, g).[17] Whoever the god may be, the type with the attributes of a dolphin and a wreath or with two dolphins is decidedly Greek. A similar deity is pictured on a coin from an unidentified Phoenician city, perhaps Azotos (Fig. 59e).[17a]

The hippocamp was comparatively uncommon in the fifth century. It occurs on red-figured vases of the earliest period, where we have again a repetition of a black-figured motif. A red-figured cylix shows an aged deity riding a hippocamp.[18] This vase is so like black-figured vases with this design (Fig. 36) that it must be of approximately the same date.

Quite different are two pairs of hippocamps on a red-figured cylix in the British Museum by the Euergides Painter.[19] They are appropriately used to separate the two scenes on the exterior of the vase, which illustrate the story of Peleus and Thetis. Riderless, they hold their heads erect as if ready for action. Except in one case, large wings

---

Triton. Pfuhl dates this cup in the mid-second century B.C. and says it is a remarkably early example of the design.

[14] *Brit. Mus. Cat. Coins, Crete and the Aegean Islands* (Wroth), pp. 51-52 and Pls. 12 and 13; I.-B. and K., Pl. XIII, 30.

[15] I.B. and K., Pl. XIII, 29.

[16] *Brit. Mus. Cat. Coins, Sicily,* p. 15, no. 89; I.-B. and K., Pl. XI, 22.

[17] *Brit. Mus. Cat. Coins, Phoenicia* (Hill), pp. 1-3 and Pl. I; I.-B. and K., Pl. XIII, 33-34.

[17a] I.-B. and K., Pl., XIII, 32.

[18] Lenormant-deWitte, *op. cit.*, III, Pl. II.

[19] *Brit. Mus. Cat. Vases,* III, E 9; Gerhard, *op. cit.*, III, 178-179.

cover the joining of the bodily parts. The fish body, which is partially obscured by the handle of the vase, is utterly unlike those of black-figured specimens. There are no scales and there is only one fin just behind the legs. The tail lacks the usual form of the conventionalized dolphin-tail. A single hippocamp is also represented on a Boetian krater in New York which belongs in the second half of the fifth century.[20]

From the first half of the century there is a clay plaque from Melos, decorated with a relief of a winged hippocamp (FIG. 60).[21] The animal is built on long slender lines and resembles the horse on Melian reliefs of the severe style. The complete absence of fins causes the equine nature of the monster to overshadow the fish nature.

During the course of the fifth century new designs with the hippocamp were introduced into Greek art. Most important is the motif of a Nereid riding a hippocamp.[22] There are several examples on red-figured vases of the period. A cylix in the Louvre shows a draped Nereid riding a hippocamp and carrying a shield.[23] A calyx krater in Vienna in the style of Polygnotos is decorated with figures of Nereids on sea-animals.[24] Although the vase is now in fragments, it is clear that there was at least one example of a hippocamp. An interesting group in relief is found on the cover of a pyxis from Eretria (Fig. 61).[25] The drawings on the vase are in the style of the Meidias Painter, and the cover has been fittingly compared to the sculptures of the Nike Parapet. The Nereid, who boldly rides astride, is dressed in a long chiton with overfold. In front of her she holds a piece of armor. The erect ears and dilated nostrils of the hippocamp give the impression of spirited action. Fins are found at the joining of the foreleg. The fish part is raised behind and ends in an s-curve.

Most interesting is the painted marble vase in the Walters Gallery in Baltimore (Fig. 62), which seems to belong to the latter half of the fifth century (cf. p. 38).[26] Poseidon and a winged Amphitrite are repre-

[20] Metropolitan Museum, 06.021.232.

[21] Jacobsthal, *op. cit.*, Fig. 34.

[22] Gang, *Nereiden auf Seetieren*, Weimar, 1907, pp. 1 ff. Gang lists examples of monuments with Nereids on sea-monsters which he believes to be fifth-century. Most scholars had previously followed Heydemann ("Die Neriden mit den Waffen des Achills", *Gratulationsschrift der Universität für das arch. Inst. in Rom*, Halle, 1879) in believing that the motif was invented by Skopas.

[23] Inghirami, *Galleria Omerica*, II, Fiesole, 1829, Pl. 171.

[24] *Wiener Vorlegeblätter*, 1890-91, Pl. IX. Cf. Jacobsthal, *op. cit.*, pp. 182 ff.

[25] Jacobsthal, *op. cit.*, Fig. 56.

[26] It seems fairly certain that the vase is genuine, though it is just possible that it has been partially repainted.

sented in a chariot drawn by two hippocamps. In front of them in the water is a figure of Triton. Each hippocamp appears to have two tails—a feature, which to the best of my knowledge, does not occur on any other ancient monument. As has already been pointed out, the greatest interest of this vase lies in the subject which, though popular in Hellenistic and Roman times, is apparently otherwise unknown at this period. The Eros flying overhead is noteworthy, although two such figures are found on a red-figured vase from Olynthos, which is probably of late fifth-century date. (*see* p. 45.)

The hippocamp was not common in the minor arts of the fifth century. A winged hippocamp, however, with a spiked fin running the whole length of its body, is represented on a silver finger-ring in the Albertinum in Dresden.[27]

Two cities in the fifth century have as a coin type a bearded deity riding a hippocamp. At Kyzikos Poseidon is represented riding the monster[28] and Tyrian coins of the second half of the fifth century show a bearded archer, probably the god Melqart, riding a hippocamp with large sickle wings (Fig. 37b).[29] In the fifth and fourth centuries, a wingless hippocamp was fairly frequent as an exergue symbol on Sicilian coins. One of the older examples is from the Siculo-Punic city of Panormus.[30] Before the close of the century, a similar symbol was in use on coins of Adranum, Akragas, Himera and Messana.[31] A coin of Sybrita in Crete, which appears to belong to the fifth century, shows a winged hippocamp (Fig. 63).[31a] This type probably alludes to the maritime activity of the city, which, though it lay in the heart of the Cretan mountains, must have extended its territory to the sea.

Despite the comparative scarcity of the hippocamp type in the fifth century, it passes through a definite development. Many examples con-

[27] *Arch. Anz.*, 1896, p. 211, no. 43.

[28] Head, *Historia Numorum*, 2nd ed., Oxford, 1911, p. 525.

[29] I.-B. and K., Pl. XI, no. 35; *Brit. Mus. Cat. Coins, Phoenicia* (Hill), pp. 229 ff. and Pls. XXVIII-XXIX. Cf. Chap. I, n. 31.

[30] *Brit. Mus. Cat. Coins, Sicily* (Poole), p. 247.

[31] Adranum: Head, *op. cit.*, p. 119; Akragas, *Brit. Mus. Cat. Coins, Sicily*, pp. 15-16, nos. 93 ff.; Himera: *Brit. Mus. Cat. Coins, Sicily*, p. 81, no. 48 and Hill, *Coins of Ancient Sicily*, London, 1903, p. 147 and Pl. VIII, no. 10; Messana: *Brit. Mus. Cat. Coins, Sicily*, p. 104, no. 52 and Hill, *op. cit.*, p. 130 and Pl. VIII, no. 14; Siculo-Punic: Hill, *op. cit.* pp. 147 ff. and Pl. X, 12.

[31a] *Illustrated London News*, March 16, 1935 (G. F. Hill). This coin is part of Mr. Seager's bequest to the British Museum. It is not only unique, but older than any other issue of the mint hitherto recorded. Cf. *Brit. Mus. Cat. Coins, Crete and the Aegean Islands* (Wroth), p. 79; Head, *op. cit.*, p. 477.

tinue to have wings. The male rider tends to die out, but the female rider comes in. Usually we find a Nereid riding a sea-animal, a motif which will be discussed more fully later. Certain new features are to be noted in fifth-century hippocamps. First of all the bodies are for the most part smooth, without scales, and have erect, crescent tails. The mane has become more of a crest or comb and the single dorsal fin is toothed or spiked. There is often a small fin back of each leg.

Fifth-century artists favored the pistrix or *ketos* rather less than the hippocamp. It is extremely rare on red-figured vases unless the sea-monster occasionally depicted in connection with the story of Peleus may be so identified. On one such vase in the British Museum a sea-creature with doglike head and forked tail is represented biting the leg of Peleus.[32] Another such monster occurs on a vase in the Louvre, attributed to the Tyszkiewics Painter.[33] Nereids riding *kete* occur occasionally on red-figured vases of the later fifth century. This subject matter is found on a red-figured cylix in the British Museum where the monster has a doglike head, pointed ears and a spiked mane.[34] A fragment of a vase in the style of the Meidias Painter shows part of a picture of a Nereid riding a *ketos*, but not enough is preserved to give us a clear idea of the monster.[35] Another example occurs on a Boeotian black-figured vase of almond-shape, dated at the very end of the century.[36]

We have an interesting example of a fifth-century *ketos* on a Melian relief of early style (Fig. 64).[37] A Nereid with armor rides on its back. The *ketos* has a spiked comb at the back of his neck, a ventral fin and crescent tail. Below are waves over which the monster is springing. The Nereid, clad in a long chiton with overfold reaching to the knees and a mantle, holds in each hand a greave. Another Melian relief of the same period represents a Nereid riding a dolphin and carrying armor and still a third may belong to this group.[38]

On a terracotta relief from Selinus Nereids are pictured riding dolphins and *kete*.[39] The *kete* are long-necked, long-eared creatures with crested manes. They have no front limbs or swimming flaps. The

[32] *Brit. Mus. Cat. Vases*, III, E 424; *Wiener Vorlegeblätter*, Series II, Pl. VI.

[33] *C.V.A.*, Louvre VI, Group III Ic, Pl. 53, 3 and 6.

[34] *Brit. Mus. Cat. Vases*, III, E 130. The monster is described in the catalogue as a hippocamp, but it has more of the characteristics of the *ketos*.

[35] Jacobsthal, *op. cit.*, Fig. 57 (in possession of Dr. Lederer in Berlin).

[36] *Arch. Anz.*, 1893, p. 87, Fig. 26a.

[37] Jacobsthal, *op. cit.*, no. 21 and Pl. 11 (Athens). See also *ibid.*, pp. 182 ff.

[38] *Ibid.*, nos. 47 and 48 and Pls. 23-24.

[39] Otto, *Terrakotten von Sicilien* (Kekule, *Die Antiken Terrakotten*, II), Berlin and Stuttgart, 1884, Pl. 57, 1 and 2. This is now in Palermo.

Nereids sit stiffly on the monsters' backs, holding armor in their outstretched hands. The archaic appearance of the piece is due to provincialism; it is dated in the forties of the fifth century.

A distinctive design with Nereids and *kete* occurs on a mosaic, recently discovered at Olynthos, which Professor Robinson dates in the latter part of the fifth century (Fig. 65).[40] Achilles, identified by an inscription, is shown seated on a rock. Thetis, also designated by an inscription, advances toward him on foot. Behind her are two Nereids riding *kete* and carrying armor. The monsters have long necks and thin, snaky bodies. A spiked fin runs the entire length of the back.

The representations of pistrices on fifth-century coins are interesting and varied. In the first half of the century a pistrix, similar to the monster already noted at Catana (*see* p. 29), was in use at Syracuse as an exergue symbol.[41] Some have thought that the Syracusan *ketos* symbolized the victory of Hiero over the Etruscans in 474 B.C.[42] From Cumae we have a type consisting of a pistrix above the characteristic Cumaean shell.[43] The monster is crested and bearded, with long snakelike body and crescent tail. The coin type with pistrices at Itanos is quite distinctive. Two monsters, crested and bearded, face each other in antithetical composition (Fig. 58b).[44] They are more like dragons or serpents than sea-horses. This type is particularly interesting, in view of the tradition that Itanos was founded by Phoenicians.[45]

These specimens give us little information about the development of the *ketos* in the fifth century. Peculiar varieties such as those found on Corinthian pinakes are lacking and there are no male riders. The type can be fairly well established as a crested, bearded monster with a crescent tail and spiked mane.

A sea-monster which appears for the first time in the fifth century is Skylla. The general assumption has always been that she came to Greece from Phoenicia, possibly in pre-Homeric times. Scholars have, therefore, been inclined to derive her name from the Phoenician word "scol" meaning "destruction."[46] Some believe it is connected with the Hebrew word "šākhal," meaning "to be robbed." Others, however, who believe the name to be Greek in origin, connect it either with σκύλαξ

[40] *A.J.A.*, XXXVIII, 1934, p. 508 and Pl. XXX.
[41] *Brit. Mus. Cat. Coins, Sicily*, pp. 154-155, nos. 67 ff.
[42] Hill, *op. cit.*, p. 58, Pl. II, 8.
[43] I.-B. and K., Pl. VIII, no. 39.
[44] *Brit. Mus. Cat. Coin, Crete*, etc., p. 51 and Pl. XIII; I.-B. and K., Pl. XII, 35.
[45] Stephanos of Byzantium, s.v. "Itanos."
[46] See Waser, *op. cit.*, pp. 1 ff.

meaning "puppy" or "whelp" or with σκύλλειν "to rend" or "flay." Marinatos, in a recent article, argues that Skylla had nothing to do with the Greek word for "dog."[47] It seems possible that we have to do with a Minoan-Mycenaean word. Skylla, the daughter of Nisos, king of Megara, fell in love with Minos while he was besieging her father's city. Minoa, the name of an island near Nisaea, the port of Megara, is further evidence of contact with Crete. Skyllaion, the name of a promontory near Troizen, may go back to the Minoan-Mycenaean period. In Crete, there was a cult of Zeus Skyllios or Skylios, named from Mt. Skyllion where he was worshipped. Little is known of this cult, but one author has considered the possibility of a connection with Skylla.[48] Further, the early Greek sculptor Skyllis and his companion Dipoinis were Cretans by birth and according to some connected with a Daidalos, who obviously cannot be the renowned Daidalos of Minoan times.

The conception of the monster Skylla may be Minoan in origin or have come from Phoenicia by way of Crete, though this can in no way be proved. Sea-faring people such as the Minoans would naturally have had tales of sea-monsters. Two monuments mentioned in another connection in fact indicate that the Minoans had tales of imaginary sea-monsters.[49] There is good reason for thinking that the localization of Skylla and Charybdis in the straits of Messina was established by the Homeric period. It may be connected with Cretan settlements in Sicily and Italy of which we have considerable evidence. The name of the city and bay of Scylletium may go back to the time.

It is clear that the Homeric Skylla had nothing to do with the Skylla pictured on classical monuments.[49a] Marinatos believes that Homer's Skylla was a kind of giant polyp.[50] This would account for her six necks and twelve feet. Skylla as conceived by Hellenic artists is only a mermaid with the foreparts of dogs joined to her body either at the waist or shoulders. This type is an invention of the Greeks.

Early representations of Skylla are found on four Melian reliefs of which the best preserved is in the British Museum (Fig. 66).[51] The fish body has one huge curve, such as is commonly seen in the case of archaic mermen, but the end is raised and curled. Except for the ribbed

[47] Marinatos, Μινωική καὶ Ὁμηρική Σκύλλα, Ἀρχ. Δελ., 1926, pp. 51 ff.
[48] Aly, *Philologus*, LXVIII, 1909, p. 430, n. 8.
[49] See p. 28. Cf. also Marinatos, *op. cit.*, pp. 57 ff.
[49a] *Odyssey*, XII, 85 ff.
[50] Marinatos, *op. cit.*, pp. 51 ff.
[51] Jacobsthal, *op. cit.*, nos. 71-74, Pls. 34-36.

ventral surface reminding us of the merman on the Northampton vase, the body is smooth (cf. Fig. 21). A comblike fin runs the entire length of the back. The human torso is held erect and is clothed in a short, sleeveless chiton. The hair is held in place by a band. The foreparts of two dogs are inorganically joined to the human body, one at the hips and the other further down. All the reliefs with representations of Skylla belong to the end of the severe style, that is, to about 460 B.C.

Somewhat similar representations of Skylla occur on some gems dated in the second half of the fifth century. A gem in the style of Dexamenos shows Skylla with one protome. She wears a short chiton, and her hair is held in place by a band as on Melian reliefs (Fig. 67).[52] Another gem in the Stosch Collection is very much like this[53] and still another, found at Ascalon and now in the Bibliothèque Nationale, differs only in minor details.[53a] In another example Skylla is nude, but otherwise similar.[54]

Skylla is exceedingly rare on red-figured vases of the fifth century. A vase, recently discovered at Olynthos, however, which is dated at the end of the fifth century, has a very unusual representation of this divinity.[55] She and several other sea-monsters are pictured carrying Nereids on their backs. So far as I know there is only one other vase showing Skylla with a Nereid and that is late South Italian.[56] On the Olynthian vase, Skylla's body is long and twists back on itself. She has a conventionalized dolphin-tail, ribbed ventral stripe and spiked dorsal fin. At her waist are the protomes of three dogs, two turned to the right and one to the left. The human part is nude and rendered in white paint. The gaily dressed Nereid on her back seems to be Thetis herself, for she is carrying a shield. Besides the Nereids, Poseidon is represented with his trident and there are three warriors, of which the nude one must be Achilles. Remarkable for the fifth century are two Erotes, commonly seen accompanying sea-creatures on Hellenistic and Roman monuments (cf. p. 71). Accordingly, if this vase is correctly dated

[52] *Ibid.*, Fig. 77; Furtwängler, *A.G.*, Pl. XIII, 32.

[53] Tölken, *Erklärendes Verzeichniss der antiken vertieft geschnittenen Steine der königlich preuszischen Gemmensammlung*, Berlin, 1835, p. 64, no. 94. Cf. also Waser, *op. cit.*, pp. 99 and 109.

[53a] Perrot and Chipiez, *op. cit.*, III, p. 442, Fig. 315.

[54] *Mon. dell'Inst.*, III, Pl. 52, Fig. 9.

[55] Robinson, *Excavations at Olynthos, Pt. V, Mosaics, Vases and Lamps of Olynthos*, Baltimore, 1933, pp. 109 ff. and Fig. 13; Pls. 78-79.

[56] Heydemann, *op. cit.*, Pl. IV and Roscher's *Lexikon*, s.v. "Nereiden."

and if the marble vase in the Walters Gallery is genuine, as it seems to be, we have in the fifth century the beginning of the sea thiasos.

A fragment of a handleless cup in Berlin of the fine style is decorated with a relief of Skylla. She is represented *de face* with protomes and two fish-tails. In her right hand she holds an oar. Skylla with two fish-tails is otherwise practically unknown before the fourth century and is in fact very uncommon before the Hellenistic age (*see* p. 76).[56a]

Coins tell us much of the evolution of the Skylla type in art.[57] She is represented fairly frequently on coins from the fifth century onward. Campanian Cumae was the first city to use her as a coin type. An example from the mid-fifth century shows Skylla clad in a chiton which reaches to the joining of the bodily parts (Fig. 68b).[58] The protome of a dog is attached to each shoulder and a third at the waist. She has a spiked dorsal fin resembling in this respect other examples noted earlier. A peculiarity of the Cumaean representation is her hand which is made to look like the claw of an animal. Cumaean coins of the later fifth century show Skylla nude and have the characteristic Cumaean mussel shell in the exergue.[59] A series of copper coins from Cumae without the mussel shell shows her with two dogs at the waist and none on the shoulders and with an oar in her left hand.[60] The type on coins of Kyzikos is very similar to the earliest examples from Cumae.[61] Skylla wears a chiton and has a protome on each shoulder. The one at the waist, however, is suppressed by the Cyzicene tunny fish.

In the middle of the fifth century, then, Skylla was always represented clothed in a short chiton which covered the joining of the parts of the body. The early gems and Melian reliefs show her with the protomai only at the girdle. On coins of the earlier period, however, she always has a protome on each shoulder as well as at the waist. The latest fifth-century coins types omit the protomai on the shoulders and represent Skylla with two protomai at the waist. Her only attribute in this period is an oar in the left hand.[62]

Of interest in the fifth century is the type of female dolphin-rider or Nereid, often represented carrying the arms of Achilles. This type is

[56a] *Berlin*, no. 2894.

[57] See Waser, *op. cit.*, pp. 98 ff.

[58] I.-B. and K., Pl. XIII, Fig. 2.

[59] *Brit. Mus. Cat. Coins, Italy*, p. 89, no. 27.

[60] *Brit. Mus. Cat. Coins, Italy*, p. 90, nos. 36-38.

[61] Head, *op. cit.*, p. 525.

[62] For further information on Skylla see also von Wahl, *op. cit.*, pp. 31-44 and p. 52.

closely related to hippocamp and *ketos* riders and should be mentioned here, although no sea-monster is involved. Two archaic terracotta statuettes prove that the type without armor is older than the fifth century. The first represents a woman, draped in a mantle with a meander border, standing on the back of a dolphin.[63] The second, which is from Locris, is a figure of a draped woman seated on a dolphin.[64] The Melian reliefs of the severe style already mentioned prove that the type with armor goes back to the first half of the fifth century.[65] The better preserved of these presents a Nereid seated sideways, as on the relief with the *ketos* described above (Fig. 64). She is dressed in a long chiton without overfold. Over her left arm she has a shield and carries a sword in her right hand. Two contemporary monuments show the same motif. The first is a marble relief from Thasos with the upper part of the Nereid missing.[66] The other is a belly lekythos in Munich by the Bowdoin Box Painter.[67] The Nereid here has a long chiton with overfold and carries a helmet and spear. Other examples on fifth-century vases include the calyx krater in Vienna mentioned above (cf. p. 40), a Nolan amphora in Leningrad assigned to the Achilles Painter,[68] the cover of a lekane in Naples[69] and the lekythos by the Eretria Painter, now in the Metropolitan Museum.[70] It is interesting to find the female dolphin-rider as a coin type at Kyzikos in the fifth century.[71]

Although relegated to a comparatively minor position in the fifth century, the sea-monster was by no means banished from Greek art. Almost all examples come from small monuments—red-figured vases, Melian reliefs, coins and a few gems. The three types of sea-monsters common in the archaic period are continued—the man-fish or merman, the hippocamp and the *ketos* or pistrix. They appear in some of the customary representations, such as the combat of Herakles with Triton and the swimming hippocamp. But new motifs are added: Triton

[63] Winter, *Die Typen der figürlichen Terrakotten* (Kekule, *Die Antiken Terrakotten*, III, 1), Berlin and Stuttgart, 1903, I, p. 162, Fig. 1.

[64] *Ibid.*, p. 162, Fig. 4.

[65] See p. 42.

[66] Jacobsthal, *op. cit.*, Fig. 53; *B.C.H.*, XLVII, 1923, Fig. 15.

[67] Jacobsthal, *op. cit.*, Fig. 54.

[68] Stephani, *Die Vasensammlung der kaiserlichen Ermitage*, St. Petersburg, 1869 (hereafter referred to as *Hermitage*), no. 1536; *Compte-Rendu*, 1865, pp. 41, 45.

[69] *Bull. Nap. Arch.*, IV, Pl. II, 1 and 2; Heydemann, *op. cit.*, Pl. V, 2.

[70] *Bulletin of the Metropolitan Museum of Art.* 1932, pp. 103 ff. and Figs. 1, 2, 3 and 6. There is also an aryballos in Athens published in Stackelberg, *Die Graeber der Hellenen*, Berlin, 1837, Pl. 36, 5.

[71] *Numismatic Chronicle*, 1887, Pl. II, 26 and 27.

carrying Theseus, the merman striking downward with his trident. Nereid riders on hippocamp, *ketos* and dolphin are added to the bearded old rider, who was probably Halios Geron. All of the sea-monsters are humanized and lose some of their dread aspects. One striking new sea-monster is invented in this period, Skylla, a mermaid with the protomes of dogs joined to her body. Particularly to be noted are the smooth unscaled bodies of the monsters, the spiky fins and crescent tails which characterize so many of these monsters in the fifth century. As stated earlier, with the exception of red-figured vases, all our examples come from Magna Graecia and Sicily, the Aegean Islands and Kyzikos. It is significant that these sites include also the type of the female dolphin-rider.

V

FISH-TAILED MONSTERS ON THE GRAVE STELAE FROM FELSINA

Many grave stelae from the Etruscan necropolis at Felsina have representations of sea-monsters, most of them dating between 510 and 360 B.C.[1] The decoration is divided into zones and the monsters usually appear in a zone above or below the main scene.

In addition to the usual type of merman such as is commonly found in Greek art,[2] the type with two long snaky tails,[3] which occurs in archaic Etruscan art also appears (cf. Fig. 44). It is to be distinguished from the "Typhon" type with snaky legs, which is represented on some of the stelae.[4]

A female monster resembling the Greek Skylla is another type of sea-divinity that occurs on the stelae. Most of these representations are of relatively late date.[5] "Skylla" is usually winged and has two tails ending in the heads of serpents.[6] The protomai, an essential characteristic of Skylla in Greece, are not necessary in the case of the Etruscan monster. In one instance their place seems to be taken by two complete dogs on either side of the picture.[7] Attributes of Skylla are the oar, the torch and the anchor.

On one of the stelae from Felsina, Skylla is undoubtedly copied from a Greek model.[8] The broad edge of the horse-shoe form of the monument is decorated with reliefs illustrating scenes from the *Odyssey*. Skylla is represented with two crossed fish-tails and a dog's protome joined to each hip. Her arms are raised and in each hand she holds a knife or a dagger. This stele probably dates in the first half of the fifth century.

Most common on the stelae is the hippocamp, represented with a few exceptions on grave stones which date between 390 and 360 B.C.

[1] Ducati, *Monumenti Antichi*, XX, 1911, pp. 541 ff.
[2] Nos. 49 (Fig. 80), 61 and 169 (Pl. V).
[3] Nos. 21 and 86.
[4] Nos. 130 (Pl. III) and 188 (Fig. 45).
[5] Nos. 12, 20, 30, 36, 42, 61, 93 (Fig. 31) and 169 (Fig. 30).
[6] Nos. 12, 30 and 169 have no wings.
[7] No. 61 (Fig. 26).
[8] Ducati, *op. cit.*, pp. 374, 699-700; Brizio, *Not. Sc.*, 1890, p. 140 and Pl. I; Elderkin, *A.J.A.*, XXI, 1917, pp. 400 ff, Fig. 2; Waser, *op. cit.*, p. 95.

Occasionally it appears alone,[9] but on one stele two hippocamps face each other in heraldic composition,[10] while on another the hippocamp and merman occur together.[11] Usually, however, the composition consists of a hippocamp and a serpent in combat (Fig. 69).[12] The hippocamp is wingless and his body with its single curve resembles many Greek and Etruscan examples.

There can be no doubt that these monsters are connected with Etruscan ideas of death and the Hereafter. Etruscan monuments show that the people were preoccupied with these ideas, especially at this time. The hippocamp found on Etruscan tomb paintings of the archaic period (Fig. 48) is probably symbolic of the voyage to the other world. Sinister figures like Skylla must have represented to the Etruscan mind some of the horrors to be faced in the passage of the soul to the West. Although most of these types show some borrowings from Greek art, the Etruscan artists have given them a distinctly native character. There is nothing about the Greek Skylla to suggest the horrors of an afterworld.

[9] Nos. 89 (Fig. 67) and 11 (Fig. 28).

[10] No. 105 (Fig. 56).

[11] No. 169 (Pl. V).

[12] Nos. 16, 21, 44, 63, 91, 92, 164 (Pl. IIb), 168 (Pl. IV) and 170 (Fig. 29).

VI

FOURTH-CENTURY REPRESENTATIONS OF SEA-MONSTERS

In general, we find fifth-century types of sea-monsters continued into the fourth century. There are no new types to record, although marine figures were more widely used in this period than in the fifth century, especially in the minor arts. There is greater elaboration in the forms of the animals; especially is this evident in the long, genuinely snaky bodies, which are often coiled and twisted. The crescent tail, so characteristic of the fifth century, is often replaced by less conventionalized forms and fins become more elaborate and fan-shaped. In some cases, particularly in the Rhodian vase of Fig. 70, we have a hint of the more fantastic monsters to come.

The outstanding work of the fourth century with representations of sea-monsters was, of course, the famous sculptured group by Skopas, which unfortunately has not survived. Pliny gives a detailed description of this work, which included figures of Poseidon, together with Thetis and Achilles and Nereids riding dolphins, hippocamps and *kete*.[1] There were Tritons and the train of Phorkys, besides fishes and other sea-creatures. According to Pliny this was the most highly esteemed of all the works of Skopas and a great achievement, "even were it the work of a lifetime". The group was finally set up in a temple built by Gnaeus Domitius in the Circus Flaminius in Rome. The base upon which it rested is still in existence. It was long assumed that the work was originally erected in Asia Minor, where Domitius had been Governor. It would then have been taken to Rome about 32 B.C. and the base would date from that time. Goethert, however, believes that Pliny was speaking of an older Domitius, who was active in Rome toward the close of the second century B.C.[2]

When we consider the importance attached to this group by Pliny, it is not strange scholars formerly believed that Skopas invented the motif of a Nereid riding a sea-animal. This was Heydemann's conclusion, drawn before the discovery of the Melian reliefs, and other early monuments on which the motif appears.[3] Other scholars have held that

[1] *N.H.*, XXXVI, 26.

[2] *Studien zur Kunst der römischen Republik*, Berlin, 1931, pp. 7 ff.

[3] Heydemann, *op. cit.*, pp. 1 ff.

the design must have originated with Zeuxis, on the ground that he had a predilection for painting monstrous creatures such as centaurs and Tritons.[4] That many monuments with this motif antedate Zeuxis and Skopas cannot now be disputed. Some of the fourth-century examples, even, are too early to be associated with Skopas. The earliest examples of the motif indicate that it was first used in Ionia and may be merely a variation of the youthful male dolphin-rider. The ultimate origin of the type may be in the Orient, though there is no real reason against the theory of a purely Hellenic origin. Skopas was probably the first artist to use the Nereid riders in an imposing work. Finally, his group cannot be certainly dated.

In reality we have no very definite evidence about the style of Skopas, but usually associate his work with the Tegea heads. There is no evidence that these were made by Skopas, though they certainly represent a new style which arose at the time when he was the architect of the temple at Tegea and probably represent his designs. In discussing the group by Skopas, we shall argue largely from the assumption that the style associated with the Tegea sculptures is that of Skopas—an assumption that may not be wholly justified. In favor of the assumption, however, is the fact that most of our copies of sea-divinities hark back to this style, though the heads show more refinement and less fire and strength in the Roman copies.

Gang has attempted to group together certain monuments, which, in his opinion, were influenced by Skopas. They belong to the fourth century or to the Hellenistic period. First of all there is a wooden sarcophagus found at Anapa in South Russia which is dated in the third century.[5] It is decorated with sculptured groups of Nereids riding sea-monsters and carrying armor.[5a] Five of these, which may have gone across the front, are superior to the others[6] and Gang believes that these were more directly influenced by Skopas. The heads of the Nereids he compares to the female head from Tegea.[7] He considers the more fantastic types of monsters, such as the sea-centauress and the long-necked *ketos*, as probably inventions of the artist. With these figures are grouped several smaller monuments of the same vicinity. There is a pair of very fine gold earrings of the fourth century with figures of Nereids

[4] von Wahl, *op. cit.*, p. 49.
[5] Gang, *op. cit.*, pp. 19 ff.
[5a] *C.-R.*, 1882-1883, Pls. III-V and pp. 48 ff.
[6] *Ibid.*, Pl. IV, 2-6.
[7] Picard, *La Sculpture antique*, II, Paris, 1926, Fig. 62.

carrying armor and riding hippocamps, artistically arranged in medallions.[8] The hippocamps have scaly bodies, twisted raised tails, and fan-shaped fins between their legs. The Nereids are completely clothed in high-girdled chitons and mantles and wear diadems and veils. A Nereid on a sea-dragon is represented on a gold plaque.[9] Another earring from Kul-Oba is adorned with microscopically small figures of Nereids on dolphins.[10] The same design, very badly preserved, is found on a gold plaque from Kertch.[11] Besides these examples from South Russia, a handsome silver mirror from Corinth, also of the fourth century, is included in his list.[12] A Nereid is represented riding a hippocamp with scaly body and a fan-shaped fin between the legs. She wears a high-girdled chiton and has a mantle about her limbs. Several coins have a very similar design, notably those of Pyrrhos of Epeiros (Fig. 37c and 94),[13] Bruttium,[13a] Larissa Kremaste[14] and Lampsakos.[15] These figures are closed, plastic and rounded, in contrast to the more unrestrained groups on South Italian vases and cistae. None of them dates before the middle of the fourth century.

Certain sculptures, some of which are fairly well-known, offer interesting material for speculation about the original marine creations of Skopas. First among these is a female figure found at Ostia, either a Tritoness or a Nereid (Fig. 71).[16] She has been compared to the Maenad of Skopas, whom she resembles with her upturned face and wild locks of hair. The sturdy torso is also similar to that of the Maenad. We can well believe that she is a copy of an original work by Skopas, softened somewhat by the Roman copyist. Certain Tritons of the Hellenistic age were perhaps influenced by Skopas, though these are

[8] *C.-R.*, 1865, Pl. II, 1 and 2. [9] *Ibid.*, 1882-1883, Pl. VII.

[10] Reinach, *Antiquités du Bosphore cimmérien*, Paris, 1892, Pl. XIX, 5.

[11] *Ibid.*, Pl. XXIV, 13.

[12] 'Εφ. 'Αρχ., 1884, pp. 74 ff., and Pl. VI, 1.

[13] *Brit. Mus. Cat. Coins, Thessaly to Aetolia* (P. Gardiner), p. 111, no. 8, Pl. XX, 11; I.-B. and K., Pl. XI, 36; Head, *op. cit.*, Fig. 183.

[13a] I.-B. and K., Pl. VII, 25.

[14] *Brit. Mus. Cat. Coins, Thessaly to Aetolia*, p. 33, Pl. VII, 1; Head, *op. cit.*, p. 300; Spink, *Numismatic Circular*, XXXVII, 1929, p. 249, Fig. 155; p. 383, Fig. 156; *Arch. Zeit.*, 1869, Pl. 23, no. 15.

[15] *Journal d'Arch. Numism.*, 1902, Pl. 15, 1. Thetis here rides a dolphin. These coins date about 412-350.

[16] *Not. Sc.*, 1913, pp. 296 ff. and p. 297, Fig. 3a and b; Beazley and Ashmole, *Greek Sculpture and Painting*, New York and Cambridge, 1932, p. 56 and Figs. 117 and 118; Lawrence, *Later Greek Sculpture*, London and New York, 1927, p. 95 (with further bibliography).

later in style. Two companion torsos in the Vatican, perhaps acroteria, are probably also derived from designs by Skopas.[17] The marine character of the divinities is certain from the fish-skin or nebris which they wear about the neck and over one shoulder. They are Roman copies of Hellenistic work dating about the time of the Ludovisi Gaul. The head of one is unfortunately missing. The better preserved figure is represented with the body held upright and the head turned toward the right shoulder. The heavy furrowed brow and slightly parted lips give a pathetic expression to the face. The pointed animal ears may be an innovation of Skopas. Two figures of Tritons from Pergamum may also be connected with the work of Skopas, who, we know, was active in Asia Minor.[18] These are dated about the time of the Great Altar. A related statue in Berlin is badly damaged, but enough of the face remains to show the deep-set eyes looking upward from beneath heavy brows.[19] Another work which belongs in this series is the Triton of the Aphrodite group in Dresden.[20] Although somewhat later in date, in the opinion of Wace and Lawrence it so greatly resembles the Orontes of the group by Eutychides that they have assigned it to the school of Antioch. The features have been much slurred over by the copyist, but the face has the same heavy brows overshadowing deepset eyes (Fig. 72). The axial twist of the body is typical of all these figures. A second century statue of Triton in Copenhagen may also be related, although the connection is more remote.[21] The face with the heavy furrowed brow has an expression of pathos. The deity has pointed ears like the Vatican torso. Although these works are all rather far removed from Skopas in time, they give us a vague, if not wholly convincing idea of what the originals may have been.[22]

[17] Amelung, *Die Skulpturen des vaticanischen Museums*, Berlin, 1903-1908, I, p. 242, Pl. 27, 105 (Galleria Lapidaria); II, p. 418, Pl. 46, no. 253; Winter, *Kunstgeschichte in Bildern, Neuearbeitung*, I, pt. 11/12 *Hellenistische Skulptur*, Leipzig, no date, Pl. 375, 2.

[18] Winter, *Altertümer von Pergamon, Die Skulpturen mit Ausnahme der Altarreliefs*, Berlin, 1908, nos. 166-167, Beiblatt 24.

[19] *Beschreibung der antiken Skulpturen* (*Königliche Museen zu Berlin*), Berlin, 1891, no. 286; Wace, *B.S.A.*, IX, 1902-1903, pp. 222 ff., Fig. 2; Lawrence, *op. cit.*, p. 101; *Arch. Anz.* 1933, p. 30, Fig. 13.

[20] Dickins, *Hellenistic Sculpture*, Oxford, 1920, p. 33, Fig. 25; Wace, *op. cit.*, pp. 221 ff., Fig. 1; Lawrence, *Journal of Egyptian Archaeology*, XI, 1925, p. 183, Pl. 20; Lawrence, *Later Greek Sculpture*, p. 101.

[21] Arndt, *La Glyptothèque Ny-Carlsberg, les monuments antiques*, Munich, 1912, p. 184, Pl. 132.

[22] For a discussion of Hellenistic Tritons in general see *Arch. Anz.*, 1933, pp.

Gang is of the opinion that Skopas was conservative in his rendering of sea-monsters; that he adhered to types already in use. It seems more likely that an original genius, such as he appears to have been, would have invented new types. Certainly, shortly after Skopas, in the Hellenistic age, new types such as the sea-centaur were in use and old types were more fantastic and bizarre. If the group was made fairly late in Skopas' career, its influence would not have been felt much before the Hellenistic period.

The "Triton" type is no longer the most common type in the fourth century.[23] Aside from the work of Skopas, the examples come from the minor arts. The merman is represented on two clay plaques, found at Dodona, and now in Athens.[24] The deity is bearded and holds an object, probably an oar, over his shoulder. About his waist is a leafy girdle, an unusual feature before the Hellenistic age. The occurrence of the merman as a coin type tended to die out, although certain cities like Karystos continued their fifth-century types. At Allifae in Samnium a merman with an oar in his right hand was employed as a reverse type early in the century.[25] On a later fourth-century coin from Corinth a tiny merman is represented behind the head of Athena, holding in his raised right hand a trident which he aims at a fish (Fig. 59d).[26]

Figures of Nereids riding sea-animals increased in popularity during the fourth century. Most representations of the hippocamp belong to this class, among them, a pedestal block from the later temple of Artemis at Ephesus.[27] The right hand in each case holds up her himation, while with her left she clasps the neck of the monster. Since we know that Skopas worked at Ephesus, it would be natural to look for his influence in these figures. Unfortunately, however, they are too badly preserved to tell us much.

One of the most interesting monuments of the period is a vase of

---

426 ff. (Greifenhagen). The Triton in Braunsberg, here published, may also belong to this group, but the head is unfortunately missing. Greifenhagen thinks it may be a Greek original of the first half of the third century B.C.

[23] Two rather curious specimens occur on Etruscan gems of the so-called "round pearl" type, Furtwängler, *A.G.*, I, Pl. XIX, nos. 70 and 74 and vol. III, pp. 191 ff. and p. 449.

[24] Carapanos, *Dodone at ses ruines*, Paris, 1878, p. 111, Pl. 61, 8. Courby, *Les vases grecs à relief*, Paris, 1922, p. 239, Fig. 40 (p. 235).

[25] I.-B. and K., Pl. XI, no. 21.

[26] *Ibid.*, Pl. XIII, no. 31.

[27] Murray, *Journal of the Royal Institute of British Architects*, 3rd series, III, pp. 48 ff. and Fig. 5. This is now in the British Museum.

Parian marble, found at Rhodes and now in Munich (Fig. 70).[28] The decoration consists in part of a frieze carved with figures of Nereids riding sea-animals and carrying armor. Four of the eleven ride hippocamps. The monsters have spiked dorsal fins running the length of the body and a small fin between the legs. Their long, smooth bodies with crescent tails are curved or twisted in snakelike fashion. The positions of the Nereids, all of whom are clothed, vary greatly, some of them being shown in back view. Furtwängler and Wolters have dated this vase about 400 B.C.[29]

A mosaic excavated at Olynthos in 1928 furnishes a splendid example of a Nereid riding a hippocamp (Fig. 73).[30] The monster has a huge fish body with spiked fin and twisted tail. The horse's head is small and fins take the place of forelegs. The Nereid, who carries a wreath, is nude except for a mantle which falls down her back. Professor Robinson gives no exact date for this mosaic, but believes that it belongs in the fourth century. New discoveries tend to show that Nereids with sea-animals were more common and more varied in the fifth and fourth centuries than was formerly supposed.

Nereid groups occur occasionally on relief vases of the fourth century. On an Attic vase, found at Kertch and now in the Scheurleer Museum at The Hague,[31] the design of a half-draped Nereid carrying a shield is found and this is repeated on the cover of a pyxis in the Louvre.[32]

There are many instances of the use of the hippocamp in the minor arts of the fourth century, some of which have already been noted, such as the design on a silver mirror from Corinth and on the gold earrings from South Russia (p. 53). With these may be coupled a bronze mirror in the Louvre.[33] The hippocamp alone is represented on a fragment of a golden quiver, also from a grave in South Russia;[34] on the sheath of a Graeco-Scythian gold fibula (Fig. 74);[35] and on a gold ring from Rhegium.[35a] Fig. 74 shows no wings or forelegs; the ring

[28] *Mon. dell'Inst.*, III, Pl. XIX.

[29] *Beschreibung der Glyptothek König Ludwigs I*, 2nd ed., Munich, 1910, pp. 181 ff., no. 203. Heydemann dated this *ca.* 220 *B.C.*

[30] Robinson, *Excavations at Olynthos*, II, Baltimore, 1930, pp. 80 ff., Fig. 205; *ibid.*, V, pp. 2 ff. and Pl. II, 11.

[31] *C.V.A.*, Pays-Bas, I, Musée Scheurleer, I, Group III L, Pl. L, nos. 3 and 4.

[32] Courby, *op. cit.*, p. 220.

[33] deRidder, *op. cit.*, no. 1711, Pl. 80.

[34] Reinach, *Antiquités du Bosphore Cimmérien*, Pl. 26, 2.

[35] *Illustrated London News*, March 3, 1934, p. 331 (Birmingham).

[35a] Furtwängler, *A.G.*, Pl. LXIV, no. 14; Marshall, *Catalogue of the Finger-Rings in the British Museum*, London, 1907, Pl. III, no. 84.

from Rhegium, large straight wings, a long curled tail and small back and belly fins.

A circular bronze matrix, which has recently come into the possession of Professor D. M. Robinson (Fig. 75), is decorated with remarkably fine marine figures.[36] It is said to have been found in southern Thessaly, not far from the site of the ancient Larissa Kremaste and the letters Λ A on the obverse indicate that it is the seal of this city. It has a double intaglio design, the one on the obverse representing Thetis on a hippocamp, the other on the reverse, Skylla swinging a trident. Just why a city twenty miles inland should have chosen these figures for its state seal and coins is not evident. Like Sybrita, its territory must have extended to the sea. The hippocamp has a smooth body and a spiked fin. Thetis wears a thin chiton with fine folds and a mantle and carries on her right arm a shield with a Medusa head. In her left hand she holds a Corinthian helmet over the horse's head. The spirited figure of Skylla will be discussed later. A hippocamp with a Nereid rider is also pictured on a bronze strigil in the Metropolitan Museum.[36a]

A Nereid riding a hippocamp is represented on several rings of the early fourth century. One of the best examples, dated around 400 B.C., is found on a silver ring from Boeotia on which a Nereid, clothed in a long Ionic chiton and mantle, carries a shield.[37] The fish body of the hippocamp is ringed like a worm and forms an s-curve, with a ring separating the body from the tail. A comblike formation runs for some distance along the animal's back. A gold ring in Boston has a very similar scene, except that the monster's body is smooth and the Nereid carries no armor (Fig. 76).[38] Two rings in the Southesk Collection repeat the design of the Boeotian ring.[39] On one of them the hippocamp has long jagged fins hanging from his chest which give him a grotesque appearance. This piece is probably Etruscan.

Coins with the hippocamp as a type or a symbol continued in many places in the fourth century, for example at Kyzikos, Himera, Messana and Tyre. In the latter part of the century a fine hippocamp with sickle wings and a long curled body with spiky dorsal fins was in use as a

[36] Robinson, "The Bronze State Seal of Larissa Kremaste, *A.J.A.*, XXXVIII, 1934, pp. 219 ff.

[36a] Richter, *Catalogue of the Bronzes in the Metropolitan Museum of Art*, p. 295, no. 857.

[37] Furtwängler, *A.G.*, Pl. LXI, no. 33.

[38] *Ibid.*, Pl. IX, no. 42.

[39] H. C. Southesk, *Cat. of the Collection of Antique Gems formed by James, IX Earl of Southesk, K.T.*, London, 1908, I, p. 129, L 4; II, p. 138, R 2.

reverse type at Syracuse (Fig. 77b).[40] In most examples he has a hanging bridle. In Lucanian Herakleia and Thurium the design of a winged hippocamp was occasionally used on coins of this period as a decoration for the helmet of Pallas.[41] The device of Thetis riding on a hippocamp occurs on coins of Larissa Kremaste.[42] They have usually been dated in the Hellenistic period, but a date in the fourth century seems probable.[42a] On some specimens the shield of Thetis is inscribed with the monogram of Achilles.

We see from these examples of hippocamps on fourth-century monuments that many characteristics of the fifth century are still common, such as the spiked comblike fin and the crescent tail. There are a few winged hippocamps, but no hippocamp with a Nereid rider has wings. The most striking change in the forms of these monsters is the tendency toward long, twisted, snaky bodies. Most of the examples come too near the beginning of the fourth century to have been influenced by Skopas.

Examples of the pistrix or *ketos* are more frequent on fourth-century monuments than earlier. They are so varied in this period that it is impossible to establish types. In the Rhodian vase, however, the fantastic monsters of later monuments are heralded. A gold plaque from the Crimaea shows a Nereid riding a *ketos* with doglike head and pectoral fins.[43] The same design is represented on several ancient gems, all of which appear to be copies of an early fourth-century original.[44] The monster has a crested doglike head, a comblike dorsal fin and a pair of front fins or swimming flaps. The Nereid is shown partly nude and holds her veil out with her hand. Some fourth-century examples of Nereids riding pistrices or *kete* are found on a grave monument from Tarentum.[45] Apparently they formed part of a frieze rather than part of a larger composition depicting the story of Peleus and Thetis. A relief in Budapest representing a woman carrying a metal breastplate is similar to these.[45a] Several Nereids on the Rhodian vase are rep-

[40] I.-B. and K., Pl. XI, no. 33.

[41] Gardner, *The Types of Greek Coins*, London, 1893, Pl. V, no. 19 and Head, *op. cit.*, pp. 48 and 72.

[42] See n. 14 above.

[42a] See n. 36 above.

[43] See n. 9 above.

[44] Furtwängler, *A.G.*, Pl. XIII, no. 43 and vol. II, p. 65; I.-B. and K., Pl. XXVI, no. 24.

[45] Klumbach, *Tarentiner Grabkunst*, Reutlingen, 1937, pp. 12 ff., nos. 49-51, Pl. 10. Cf. also *ibid.*, p. 63.

[45a] *Ibid.*, p. 24, no. 122, Pl. 22.

resented riding pistrices (Fig. 70), but these animals are more closely related to the hippocamp.[45b] Their pointed doglike heads and crested manes, however, make their true nature unmistakable.

A few cities in Magna Graecia and Sicily used the pistrix on coins of the fourth century. A hemidrachma of Akragas has as a reverse type a crab and beneath, a pistrix with spiked fin and open, denticulated jaws.[46] A different type occurs on a coin of the Messapian city of Valetium, where the pistrix seems to have the body of an ordinary fish and a head of rather canine appearance.[47]

One of our most beautiful representations of Skylla appears on the reverse of the seal of Larissa Kremaste (Fig. 75).[48] She has a nude upper body and flying hair. The fish part is scaly, with a spiked fin and bifurcated tail. At her waist are the foreparts of two ferocious dogs, one looking forward, the other down. With her left hand she swings a trident; in her right she holds a cuttle fish.

Skylla occurs on two fourth-century grave reliefs found at Tarentum.[48a] These are interesting because they show some features which are unusual in the fourth-century type of Skylla. The finny girdle about the hips, found in both examples, is rare before the Hellenistic age. The two-tailed Skylla, shown on the second relief, was also uncommon at this time. In this relief we have besides an early example of the so-called motif of Skylla seizing the companions of Odysseus (cf. p. 75). The first relief has been connected with the school of Skopas, the second with the school of Timotheos.[48b]

Another unusual representation of Skylla is found on a bronze mirror handle in the Louvre.[49] This was probably also made in Tarentum in the fourth century. She is nude with two fish-tails each ending in the head of a sea-dragon. On each side is a dog-protome. Her only attribute is an oar which she brandishes over her head. About her waist is a leafy girdle and the whole figure seems to grow out of this leafy formation. A clothed Skylla is represented in profile on two bronze plaques, however, with one tail ending in a dragon-head.[50] In other respects she resembles

[45b] See n. 28 above.

[46] I.-B. and K., Pl. XII, 34.

[47] *Arch. Zeit.*, XI, 1853, Pl. LVIII, no. 17.

[48] See n. 36 above.

[48a] Klumbach, *op. cit.*, p. 3, no. 8, Pl. 1 and p. 24, no. 120, Pl. 21.

[48b] *Ibid.*, pp. 70, 76.

[49] deRidder, *op. cit.*, II, no. 1686, Pl. 76.

[50] Reinach, *Stat.*, II, p. 413, no. 4 (Collection Gréau 250); *Gaz. Arch.*, 1880, pp. 48 ff. (Copenhagen).

the Skylla pictured on South Italian and Sicilian coins (cf. Fig. 68a-d) so that it seems probable that the plaques were made in Southern Italy in the fourth century.

Skylla was frequently represented on fourth-century coins, particularly in the West. She was more popular in Italy, however, than in Sicily. We find her represented beneath the crab on an early fourth-century coin at Akragas (Fig. 68d).[51] Her arm is raised as if beckoning and her hair streams behind her. As on late fifth-century coins she is nude and has the protomai of two dogs at her waist. A distinctive feature is the fimbriated character of her tail and of the front fins behind the protomai. On coins of Allifae, which date in the first half of the fourth century and which must be dependent on Cumae (*see* p. 46), Skylla is represented nude and with a spiked dorsal fin. The earlier examples have the protomai on the shoulders as well as at the waist (Fig. 68a).[52]

In the fourth century a figure of Skylla was often used to decorate the helmet of the deity or hero represented on the coin.[53] She is often shown slinging a stone or holding a *χερμάδιον* in each hand. Sometimes she is shouldering an oar or a trident and frequently she has one hand raised in an attitude of beckoning. Most of the examples come from Italy, but coins from Pharsalos in Thessaly show Skylla on the helmet of Athena.[54] The first city to use Skylla as a helmet decoration was Thurium in the first half of the fourth century.[55] Here she is depicted on the helmet of Pallas with her arm raised as if beckoning. The spiked fin and two protomai seem to be universal characteristics at this time, while the tail is conventionalized into two crescents joined end to end. The body is smooth and curved. The same device is later used on coins of Herakleia.[56] Tarentine coins with this type are relatively late and of small denomination.[57] On a gold coin of Metapontum a figure of Skylla decorated the helmet of the hero, Leukippos.[58] As on late fifth-century monuments, Skylla on these coins is always represented nude and with protomai at her waist. The only new features are the attitudes of beckoning, shouldering an oar or slinging a stone.

[51] I.-B. and K., Pl. XIII, no. 4.
[52] *Ibid.*, Pl. XIII, no. 1.
[53] Waser, *op. cit.*, pp. 102 ff.
[54] *Brit. Mus. Cat. Coins, Thessaly to Aetolia*, p. 43, Pl. IX, 10.
[55] Gardner, *op. cit.*, Pl. V, nos. 17-18.
[56] *Ibid.*, Pl. XI, no. 13 and Pl. V, no. 44.
[57] *Brit. Mus. Cat. Coins, Italy*, pp. 201 ff.
[58] *Ibid.*, p. 238.

The Rhodian vase illustrates well the change in the type of the female or Nereid dolphin-rider (Fig. 70). She no longer rides perched on the animal's back, but rather clings to his body with both arms. We shall see this tendency carried further on later monuments.

Other fish-tailed types are extremely rare before the Hellenistic age. There is in the Metropolitan Museum, however, a bronze relief from a utensil with a representation of a draped Nereid riding a sea-goat.[59] This is dated in the fourth century.

[59] No. 25.78.88.

VII

LATER RED-FIGURED VASES WITH DESIGNS OF MARINE MONSTERS

Examples of sea-monsters on late vase paintings come either from the region of the Crimaea in South Russia or from Southern Italy. Most of the South Russian specimens are found on fish-plates on which the story of Europa is illustrated. She is accompanied by a thiasos of sea-creatures including deities in the form of mermen and Nereids on hippocamps.[1]

The merman occurs most commonly as part of a thiasos. He is still a venerable deity with a beard, but in contrast to the clothed merman of the earlier part of the fifth century he is shown nude with a complete human torso.[2] On the ventral surface is a large pair of fins. His attributes are an oar and a trident.[3] A mermaid also appears on one of the fish-plates.[4]

A Nereid riding a hippocamp is always part of the thiasos on Kertch vases which picture the legend of Europa. The monster's legs are extended and his head is held high as if galloping at full speed. Ordinarily he has a horse's mane, though occasionally a crested or comblike fin more typical of the *ketos* is found.[5] Besides the fish-plates a few later vases picture the same motif.[6]

The *ketos* is extremely rare on vases from South Russia and occurs on none of the Europa plates. On a late vase from Juz-Oba a Nereid is represented riding a *ketos* with spiked mane and dotted body with fin-like front limbs and fimbriated fish-tail.[7]

By far the greater number of sea-monsters of this period are to be found on South Italian vases, particularly on vases of the Apulian class. They give local color to some mythological scene, such as Perseus with

[1] See *Appendix*, pp. 98 ff.

[2] *C.-R.*, 1880, p. 106. See also *Hermitage*, no. 1799.

[3] For another fragment on which the merman carries a trident see *C.-R.*, 1876, Pl. V, no. 14.

[4] *Hermitage*, no. 1800. Cf. *C.-R.*, 1866, p. 82.

[5] *C.-R.*, 1876, Pl. V, no. 11.

[6] *Hermitage*, no. 1621; *Mém. de la Soc. Arch. de St.-Pétersbourg*, I, Pl. 20 (third century); *Hermitage*, no. 2023; *C.-R.*, 1863, *Title Vignette*.

[7] *C.-R.*, 1863, *Title Vignette*.

Andromeda,[8] Phrixos and Helle crossing the Hellespont,[9] or Peleus carrying off Thetis.[10] In contrast to the monsters on Kertch or South Russian vases, which follow the Attic tradition, the South Italian specimens seem highly fantastic, and are remarkable for their variations. They bear a strong resemblance to those depicted on Etruscan mirrors and cistae. The Etruscan examples, however, were probably influenced by the South Italian, although certain types such as the two-tailed merman were invented in Etruria. The Nereid rider remains the favorite motif.

We find the merman type occasionally on South Italian vases. On a vase of early date, a merman, human to the waist and with a scaly fish-body, unusual at this time, is seen aiming a spear at some invisible adversary.[11] A merman and mermaid, each wearing a wreath and holding an oar, are represented on a Campanian hydria on the point of clasping hands.[12] Two Bacchic scenes on a South Italian vase in Palermo are separated by figures of a merman and Skylla.[13] Better known is the merman on a calyx krater signed by the painter Assteas.[14] The theme of this painting is the story of Phrixos and Helle, and the merman forms part of a group of sea-monsters in the background. He holds a trident and turns to look back at Skylla. He shares with the mermen on Kertch vases the double belly line and large pair of fins at the joining of the fish and human body; with South Italian, the dotted fish body. The head of a merman, inscribed "Tritun", is preserved on a fragment of an Etruscan plate.[15] He holds a conch to his lips and accompanies a Nereid on a *ketos*.

The hippocamps on South Italian vases are so varied that generalization is difficult. Certain characteristics, however, stand out. The fish's body and sometimes the horse's body have inner markings of rings and

[8] Naples, *Santangelo*, 708; *Mon. dell'Inst.*, IX, Pl. 38; Langlotz, *op. cit.*, no. 855 and Pl. 242.

[9] *Naples*, no. 3412; *Wiener Vorlegeblätter*, Series B, Pl. II; Rayet and Collignon, *Histoire de la céramique grecque*, Paris, 1888, p. 314, Fig. 117.

[10] *Mon. dell'Inst.*, XII, Pl. 15; *C.V.A.*, Musée Czartoryski, Pl. 48; Beazley, *Greek Vases in Poland*, Oxford, 1928, pp. 72-74, Pls. 31, 32, 1-2.

[11] Langlotz, *op. cit.*, no. 828 and Pl. 239 (Würzburg).

[12] Metropolitan Museum, New York, no. Gr 998. Cf. Roscher's *Lexikon*, s.v. "Triton", Fig. 9, for a South Italian skyphos where a merman and mermaid are pictured facing.

[13] *Mon. dell'Inst.*, IV, Pl. 10.

[14] See n. 9 above.

[15] Inghirami, *Monumenti Etruschi*, Fiesole, 1824, V, Pl. 55, Fig. 8.

dots.[16] A horse's mane is the rule, but crested manes are not uncommon. Usually the monsters have the forelegs of a horse with a pair of fins directly behind them. In one or two cases fins take the place of legs. The tail may be a conventionalized fork or a crescent, or even a large flappy fin. There are only isolated instances of winged hippocamps.[17]

Usually the hippocamp has a Nereid rider. Often the figures form part of a mythological scene. Skylla fighting with a hippocamp (Fig. 78a),[18] the combat of Peleus and Thetis (Fig. 79),[19] Perseus rescuing Andromeda in the presence of Nereids riding hippocamps (Fig. 80),[20] Orpheus in Hades,[21] all are found in this connection. The familiar scene of Thetis and the Nereids riding on hippocamps and bringing armor recurs. They differ little among themselves except in the speckled, scaly or snaky bodies and in the use of fins for legs occasionally.[22]

Besides the vases of the regular South Italian class, a krater of Faliscan fabric pictures the Dawn with Kephalos (?) riding in a chariot over the ocean, which is symbolized by a hippocamp, a *ketos* and a dolphin (Fig. 81).[23] Perhaps the journey of the soul to the other world is suggested. The hippocamp, with ribbed ventral surface and spotted body, resembles South Italian specimens. In addition, a Faliscan stamnos has plastic handles in the form of two hippocamps with tails entwined (Fig. 82).[24] The hippocamp also occurs occasionally on Etruscan vases of this period.[25]

The *ketos* shares some of the functions and characteristics of the hippocamp. Inner markings such as spots, dots or rings are very common (Fig. 78b). He often serves as a steed for a Nereid or forms part of a sea thiasos. He appears to have almost as many variations as the hippocamp, but these are evident in the type of long snout, horned nose, snaky neck or flappy acanthuslike tail.[26] There are also occasional examples of the *ketos* on Faliscan and Etruscan vases (Fig. 81).[27]

Skylla is never represented on vases from South Russia, but is com-

[16] Langlotz, *op. cit.*, no. 821 and Pl. 238 (Würzburg).
[17] *Naples*, no. 3252. Cf. Beazley, *J.H.S.*, XLVII, 1927, p. 228, n. 25.
[18] See n. 16 above.
[19] See n. 10 above.
[20] See n. 8 above.
[21] *Naples*, no. 3222; *Mon. dell'Inst.*, VIII, Pl. 9.
[22] For other examples see *Appendix*, p. 99.
[23] *C.V.A.*, Villa Giulia, III, Group 4 Br, Pls. 5, 7, with full bibliography.
[24] Boston 07.862 c6146.
[25] *Brit. Mus. Cat. Vases*, IV, F 491 and 521; *Naples* 2467.
[26] See *Appendix*, p. 102.
[27] See n. 23 above.

paratively frequent on those of South Italy, where the rocky coast line called for her presence. In general the fishy part resembles that of other South Italian sea-monsters. Inner markings such as dots and rings and the double belly line are like those of other South Italian monsters (Fig. 78b).[28] A plastic representation of Skylla is found on several Apulian askoi (cf. Fig. 83).[29] The protomai are arranged one on either side of the neck of the vase, while from her back comes a long spotted tail which runs along the top of the askos. A strange monster is found on a volute krater in Naples where a bearded, male "Skylla" is represented contending with warriors.[30] He has two fish-tails and the protomai of three dogs. He wears a crown and has a mantle about one arm, while with the other he aims an oar at one of his adversaries. Beazley dates this vase near the end of the fourth century and considers the work provincial.

To sum up: on late fifth-century and early fourth-century vases from South Russia and Southern Italy, the Nereid rider of hippocamps and *kete* is very common. She may be a spectator of some mythological combat, such as that involving Perseus and Andromeda, Peleus and Thetis, Phrixos and Helle. All of the monsters grow more fantastic, and spotted and ringed bodies, coiled, twisted and spiny tails lend a more exotic air to the scenes and foreshadow the baroque. The sea thiasos plays an important rôle, but the marine figures are merely subsidiary witnesses to events and are introduced to lend additional atmosphere to some marine tale.

[28] See *Appendix*, p. 104.

[29] Boston 99.541 c808; *Brit. Mus. Cat. Terracottas*, D 203. *C.V.A.*, Brit. Mus. VII, IV Da, Pl. 17, 3; *Annali*, 1857, Pl. G.

[30] *Museo Borbonico*, XIII, Pl. 58 (*Naples*, no. 1767); Beazley, *J.H.S.*, XLVII, 1927, pp. 228 ff., Fig. 5. The figures resemble some found on Etruscan cinerary urns (*see* p. 82, n. 13, 6). Heydemann calls this group Proteus and Menelaos.

VIII

REPRESENTATIONS ON LATE ETRUSCAN BRONZES AND JEWELLERY

Most of the Etruscan examples of sea-monsters of the fourth and third centuries occur on bronzes and Praenestine cistae, many of the designs of which show a close relationship to those found on South Italian vases. In the case of the mirrors, various types of sea-monsters may figure in the picture, but more often they are merely engraved as filling ornament in the exergue space above the handle. The cistae, which were nearly all found in or near the ancient town of Praeneste, were apparently toilet boxes. With one or two exceptions, only the covers and not the cistae themselves were decorated with figures of sea-monsters.

The merman was not much used in Etruscan art of this period.[1] Only one cista offers a certain example of the ordinary type,[2] although some of the unillustrated specimens with "Triton" may picture the type.[3] On the other hand, there are several examples of the two-tailed merman. This type is used decoratively with hippocamps on two cistae covers.[4] The main frieze of a cista in the Loeb Collection also shows the Etruscan love for strange hybrid demons. Poseidon appears in combat with a winged sea-deity whose body ends in two scaly fish-tails, the ends of which resemble conventionalized prickly leaves.[5] On the body of another cista, recently excavated, Herakles is pictured fighting a beardless giant with two fish-tails.[6] Both these scenes formed part of a gigantomachy, and the scene on an Etruscan mirror where Athena is depicted fighting a two-tailed sea-monster is a composition similar to

[1] In the Louvre (deRidder, *op. cit.*, II, no. 2638, Pl. 96) is a figure of a bearded merman seizing a nude youth. This piece originally formed part of the decoration of an amphora. It probably belongs in the early fourth century. Another group in Dresden consists of a bearded merman and an armed man whom he holds against his body (*Annali*, 1874, Pl. K). This is difficult to date. It may be of the fifth century.

[2] *Museo Borbonico*, XIV, Pl. 40.

[3] *Bull. dell'Inst.*, 1866, p. 79; p. 80, VII; p. 81, VIII.

[4] *Mon. dell'Inst.*, Suppl. Vol., Pls. 17-18, 19-20.

[5] Sieveking, *Die Bronzen der Sammlung Loeb*, Munich, 1913, pp. 82 ff., Pl. 41; Chase, *A.J.A.*, XV, 1911, pp. 465 ff., Pl. 12; *Not Sc.*, 1933, p. 190, Fig. 9b.

[6] *Not. Sc.*, 1933, pp. 186 ff., Fig. 8 and Pl. 3 (Battaglia).

the well-known combat of Athena and the giant.[7] The two-tailed mermen on Etruscan mirrors are sometimes represented holding dolphins or other fish.[8] Around the waist is a spiked girdle from beneath which appear two slender, coiled fish bodies terminating in spreading flowerlike tail fins. Sometimes we find this type in the exergue or as a medallion in the center of a mirror in a highly conventionalized composition.[9] There are also occasional examples of the type in Etruscan jewellery. Each end of a gold wreath in the British Museum is stamped with the design of a bearded merman with two fish-tails and a fish in either hand.[10] This piece is dated in the third century.

There is some evidence that the Etruscans sometimes mixed the types of the two-tailed merman and the snake-footed giant for which they always had a predilection. For instance, the fish-tailed monster shown in combat with Athena on the mirror mentioned above (p. 66) is clearly a variant of the snake-footed giant with Athena represented on Greek monuments.[11] On another mirror we have the reverse: a snake-footed deity is depicted with small fins on his "thighs" and with a dolphin in either hand.[12]

There are also instances of curious female monsters with two tails. One forms the decoration of an exergue and is represented holding in each hand one end of a laurel wreath which surrounds the mirror.[13] Her tails are crossed and end in comblike fins. She has wings of a peculiar finlike character. Two dolphins on either side of the figure complete the composition. This monster has generally been called Skylla, although she lacks the distinguishing protomai. Another female monster, probably also an Etruscan variation of Skylla, is found on a cista cover with other fantastic sea-creatures.[13a] She has the upper body of a woman and two fish-tails ending in dragons' heads. In each hand she holds a

[7] Gerhard, *Etruskische Spiegel*, Berlin, 1843-1897, IV, Pl. 286, 1; Chase, *op. cit.*, Fig. 3.

[8] *Etruskische Spiegel*, V (ed. by Klügmann and Körte), Pl. 54. Cf. Royal Ontario Museum, CA. 370.

[9] *Ibid.*, IV, Pl. 404; I, Pl. 30, 2.

[10] Marshall, *Catalogue of the Jewellery, Greek, Etruscan and Roman, in the British Museum*, London, 1911, no. 2300, Fig. 81 and Pl. L. Cf. *Not. Sc.*, 1900, p. 554, Fig. 2 for a similar wreath discovered in a third-century sarcophagus at Perugia.

[11] Smith, *J.H.S.*, IV, 1883, pp. 90 ff.

[12] Gerhard, *op. cit.*, I, Pl. 76. See also *ibid.*, IV, Pl. 297. Cf. p. 32 and p. 32, n. 9.

[13] *Mon. dell'Inst.*, VI, Pl. 29, Fig. 1; Gerhard, *op. cit.*, IV, Pl. 333; *Brit. Mus. Cat. Bronzes*, no. 695.

[13a] *Museo Borbonico*, XIV, Pl. 40.

small sea-serpent. Approximately contemporary with these is a bronze vase-handle in the Metropolitan Museum composed of a palmette surmounted by the figures of two mermaids supporting a warrior.[14] Each monster has two tails tightly entwined and fins on her "thighs".

Two Etruscan mirrors are decorated with representations of Skylla.[15] In both she has a spiked girdle below which are two long fish bodies and the foreparts of three dogs. In one example she has two fish-tails, but in the other their place is taken by two dragons' heads (*see* p. 59). In both cases she is pictured brandishing an oar in her raised hand. The type of Skylla with protomai is definitely copied from Hellenistic Greek art.

The hippocamp is represented on many archaic Etruscan monuments. The type found on the cistae and mirrors is apparently related to the type seen in South Italian vase painting. Certain differences such as the more abundant inner markings may be due to the different technique (cf. Fig. 84). Fins on the horse's belly are common and occasionally pectoral fins are found in the place of legs. No crested manes occur and the continuous spiked dorsal fin is unusual. The double belly line is even more the rule than on vases and is practically always filled in with cross lines. There are many Nereid riders both with and without armor and they are frequently represented clinging to the monster's body with one arm around his neck (Fig. 84).[16]

On Etruscan mirrors the hippocamp is sometimes used as filling ornament in the exergue. It usually forms part of an antithetical composition with a *ketos* or another hippocamp. In examples combined with the figure of a Nereid, the monster and Nereid occupy the entire space. Two specimens with a youthful winged god as rider probably offer the oldest examples of Eros riding a hippocamp. Hippocamps on mirrors do not differ stylistically from those on cistae, except that the drawing of the exergue figures is sometimes rather sketchy.[16a]

A few pieces of Etruscan jewellery show the hippocamp as a decoration. A pendant of a necklace is adorned with a figure of a winged Nereid riding a hippocamp with a crested mane.[17] The monster has

[14] No. 25.78.53. For an almost identical handle see *Collection J. Gréau, Catalogues des bronzes antiques*, Paris, 1885, p. 32, no. 153, p. 33 (vignette).

[15] Klügmann-Körte, *op. cit.*, Pls. 52-53. None of the cistae with Skylla has been published. For the unpublished examples, see *Bull. dell'Inst.*, 1866, p. 43, pp. 79 ff.

[16] See *Appendix*, p. 99 ff.

[16a] See *Appendix*, 100 ff.

[17] Marshall, *op. cit.*, no. 2284, Fig. 74.

spreading pectoral fins wrongly termed wings in the publication. On two semi-elliptical plaques of very thin gold a nude youth is represented kneeling, with his arms placed beneath the necks of two hippocamps.[18] The monsters face outward and below each is a serpent. A brooch in the British Museum also has the form of a hippocamp.[19]

The hippocamp is rare on Etrusco-Italic coins. There is, however, in the British Museum an example of a coin with a hippocamp from an unknown Etruscan city (Fig. 77a).[20]

The *ketos* is not found on Etruscan monuments of the archaic period and was probably introduced later from Southern Italy. Many specimens resemble in type those represented on South Italian vases. More abundant inner markings and greater precision of line are evident. The *kete* on cistae have canine heads with crested manes and long snouts (Fig. 84). The beard is usual but not essential. Pectoral fins are common but some specimens have horse's hoofs or the claws of an animal.

On mirrors, the *ketos*, like the hippocamp, is sometimes represented in the exergue. Once the figure of a *ketos* is introduced for local color, as a scene with Poseidon and Amymone. Only occasionally is it represented on a mirror as the main decoration and just once with a Nereid rider. Although often carelessly and indifferently drawn, the examples on the mirrors do not vary greatly from those on the cistae.[21]

The types of sea-monsters depicted on later Etruscan monuments correspond roughly to the Greek. As in the archaic period, however, the Etruscans did not confine themselves to a few fixed types. That they mixed the hippocamp and *ketos* types is evident in some examples. The popularity of the hippocamp here as in the archaic period is very striking. Both this monster and the *ketos* are related to the Greek types found on South Italian vases. Sometimes they have a mythological setting. In the case of the human monsters there is considerable modification. Perhaps under the influence of the snake-footed demon, human types with two long snaky tails become popular. Apparently the same monster is occasionally represented with two snake-heads in place of the fish-tails. Many of these partially human sea-monsters have wings such as Etruscan artists were always fond of giving both to their human and animal figures. As we shall see in the next chapter, the youthful, beardless merman occurs also in Hellenistic Greek art.

[18] *Ibid.*, nos. 2318-9, Pl. XLVII.
[19] *Brit. Mus. Cat. Bronzes*, no. 2158.
[20] *Brit. Mus. Cat. Coins*, Italy, p. 397. I.-B. and K., Pl., XI, 32.
[21] See *Appendix*, p. 103.

IX

THE FISH-TAILED MONSTER ON HELLENISTIC MONUMENTS

Hellenistic artists were not content with four or five types of sea-monsters, but used their fancy freely in the invention of new and strange combinations. Many of the types are decidedly bizarre and some of them may have arisen under the influence of Skopas. The baroque tendencies which many examples exhibit are more characteristic of the style usually associated with Skopas than of any other sculptor of the fourth century.

In addition to examples found in the minor arts, sculptured reliefs, including the gigantomachy of the Great Altar at Pergamum, must be considered. On the whole, the artists' conceptions of the monsters tend to be more trivial and playful, the monsters less dignified. With a few exceptions sea-monsters were not used in mythological scenes on Hellenistic monuments: a large number of examples have a purely decorative function. Nereids on sea-creatures were very popular, only in this period they often ride mermen and ichthyocentaurs as well as hippocamps and *kete*. An evident quality of abandon present in some specimens, recalls Bacchic thiasoi with satyrs and maenads. The most noticeable changes in the form of the merman and of many other types of this time are the girdle of leaves which surrounds the body at the point of transition between the human and fish bodies, the jagged leaflike wings and the long coiled, serpentine fish body with the tail-fin held erect.

The ichthyocentaur, sometimes called a sea-centaur or centaurotriton,[1] is an invention of the Hellenistic age. This monster has the torso of a human being, the chest and forelegs of a horse and the tail of a fish. The ancients apparently did not distinguish between this monster and the ordinary merman as the sea-centaur on the frieze of the Great Altar at Pergamum is labeled "Triton". Although the figure from this frieze is not completely preserved, the most essential characteristics are discernible.[2] The hoofs are surrounded by two rows of small leafy fins. The joining of the horse and fish parts is covered with a double girdle of acanthus leaves. The fish-tail comes out of a calyx of pointed fins. This

[1] Term *ichthyocentaur* first used by Tzetzes, *Lykophr.*, 34.

[2] Winnefeld, *Altertümer von Pergamon, Die Frieze des groszen Altars*, Berlin, 1910, III, 2, pp. 84 ff. and Pl. 21.

Triton has wings of jagged leafy appearance, similar to those of his girdle. The face is unfortunately missing, but he appears to have been bearded.

A small frieze from Pergamum is decorated with a continuous composition of sea-centaurs fighting with sea-animals. The figures are arranged in pairs facing each other in single combat (Fig. 85).[3] In one of the better preserved groups a beardless ichthyocentaur is represented with a mantle wrapped about his arm which is thrust forward for protection against a sea-bull. He is further defending himself with a spear held in his raised right hand. He has the leafy girdle typical of the period. This frieze is dated in the time of the kings. A small fragment of a similar frieze shows part of an ichthyocentaur engaged in an encounter with a winged monster.[4]

A frieze from Lamia of the period of the Diadochi[5] is filled with sea-creatures of all types (Fig. 90). The ichthyocentaur resembles the mermen depicted on the same monument, except for his horse's legs. On a bit of the relief not pictured here he holds a piece of drapery which is spread over his back as a seat for a nude Nereid rider. A small Eros sits on another curve of his tail. Another example of the type, this time carrying a Silen, is found in a group of the Pergamenian school at Versailles, dated about 200 B.C.,[6] the head of which has been compared to the head of a kneeling Gaul in the Louvre; another group in the Vatican, largely restored, consists of a sea-centaur carrying off a maiden.[7] Two Erotes ride on the monster's tail. This piece is generally dated in the first century B.C.

Two marble heads of the second century, now in the Vatican, may have belonged to sea-centaurs. One with sea-weed in his hair, horns on his head and a dolphin in his beard was considered by Brunn in his *Götterideale* to be a typical personification of the sea.[8] The face is calm, with the lips slightly parted, whereas the second head has a heavy wrinkled brow.[8a] The occasional examples of the type found

[3] Winter, *Altertümer von Pergamon, Die Skulpturen mit Ausnahme der Altarreliefs*, VII, 2, Berlin, 1908, pp. 297 ff. and Pl. XXXIX, no. 385A.

[4] *Ibid.*, p. 303, no. 390.

[5] Svoronos, *Das Athener Nationalmuseum*, German edition by Dr. Barth, Athens, 1908, p. 237, Pl. 33a and b.

[6] Greifenhagen, *Röm. Mitt.*, XLV, 1930, pp. 155 ff., Fig. 6 and Pls. 50-51.

[7] Amelung, *op. cit.*, II, p. 386, no. 228, Pl. 43.

[8] Winter, *Kunstgeschichte in Bildern, Neuearbeitung*, I, pt. 11/12, *Hellenistische Skulptur*, Pl. 375, Fig. 1. Cf. Brunn, *Griechische Götterideale*, Munich, 1893, pp. 68 ff., Pl. VI.

[8a] Winter, *Kunstgeschichte in Bildern*, Pl. 375, Fig. 2.

among the minor arts may be illustrated by a small bronze figure in the Louvre on which a bearded sea-centaur is shown galloping to the left.[9] This originally formed part of a handle and was found in Lower Egypt.

Besides the above examples there are some unusual variations of the centaur type. The famous frieze of Domitius, formerly considered Graeco-Roman, is now dated in the Hellenistic period (*see* p. 51).[10] It formed the base upon which Skopas' group is assumed to have rested in the Circus Flaminius in Rome. The subject is the wedding of Poseidon and Amphitrite, accompanied by Nereids on sea-animals. One of the bizarre types found here is an ichthyocentaur with crab's claws in the place of horse's legs. Three sea-centaurs with Nereids on their backs (p. 52)[11] also occur on the wooden sarcaphagus from Anapa mentioned earlier. Only one is of the ordinary male type. The other two are females of rather exotic appearance whose torsos seem to grow out of a flowerlike calyx. Both carry armor. The fish bodies are long, thin and curled. The Nereids are completely clothed in long chitons.

Another variation of the merman, new to Greek art in the Hellenistic period, though found early in Etruria, is the type with two fishtails. The "Triton" in Dresden, mentioned above in connection with Skopas, is of this character (Fig. 72; *see* p. 54). On the frieze of Domitius, the chariot of Poseidon and Amphitrite is drawn by two mermen, one of this type (*see* p. 66) who blows a conch shell and a second who carries a lyre and has winglike fins in place of the girdle. The two-tailed mermen sometimes closely resemble the snake-footed giants depicted on Hellenistic monuments. This is the case with the "Triton" in Copenhagen (p. 54). On a gem in Berlin a youthful two-tailed merman holding a trident and an oar, rests on his "knees" with the tails coiled up on either side as in many representations of the giants (Fig. 86).[12]

The ordinary merman is perhaps more frequent than in the period immediately preceding, but his position is humbler. He no longer has the rank of a god, but is rather more on a footing with hippocamps and pistrices. For the first time, he is frequently represented with a rider, who may be either a Nereid or a chubby Eros.

[9] deRidder, *op. cit.*, no. 358, Pl. 30.

[10] *Ant. Denk.*, III, Pl. XII. This relief is partially illustrated in many other places. Cf. the marble cup recently discovered in Rome (*Not. Sc.*, 1935, pp. 69 ff., Pls. V-VII), which greatly resembles the relief in its style.

[11] *C.-R.*, 1882/3, Pl. III, 1, 4 and 5.

[12] Furtwängler, *A.G.*, Pl. XXXIII, 40.

A distinctive example of the Hellenistic period is seen in a pair of mermen carved in relief on a grave stele from the Peiraeus (Fig. 87).[13] The figures are antithetically grouped below the principal relief. The human body seems to grow out of a calyxlike fish body. The attributes are the oar and the conch shell. Here the mermen are probably symbolic of the voyage of the deceased.

On a number of well-known Hellenistic reliefs a frieze of Nereids riding sea-monsters is found, *e.g.*, on the piece of drapery from the great sculptured group at Lykosura, known to be the work of Damophon of Messene (Fig. 88).[14] It is dated in the second century B.C. One of the monsters is a merman with a long twisted snaky body and leafy girdle. The Nereid rests one arm on the shoulder of the merman who turns his youthful beardless face toward her. The erotic element becomes more pronounced on these monuments of late date.

A sandal on a marble foot, which was originally part of a Greek statue, is decorated with a frieze of dolphins and mermen with Amorini (Fig. 89).[15] One would like to believe the sandal that of Aphrodite, for whom the designs would be appropriate. The style is not so extravagant as in the Roman Imperial period, but the childish forms of the Amorini prove it to be later than the fourth century. The piece has been assigned purely on stylistic criteria to Damophon of Messene, and the three mermen bear some resemblance to the Lykosura monster. Their attributes are typical of the period—a shallow basket, a paddle and a conch shell. For the first time in the Hellenistic age we have Triton blowing his horn, but he is not always an aged Triton as we shall see.

On the small frieze from Lamia mermen appear several times (Fig. 90; cf. p. 71).[16] In form they are close to the specimens on the drapery and the sandal. One blows a large conch shell; another has a whip with which he drives a hippocamp; still a third holds a trident in one hand and supports an amphora on his shoulder. The Nereid, of whom only the upper part is preserved, carries a large basket filled with fruits.

A torso of a merman in Braunsberg may be a Greek original of the first half of the third century (cf. Chap. VI, n. 22). The head is missing and the body broken off just below the navel, but the transition to

[13] Brückner, *Ath. Mitt.*, XIII, 1888, p. 377, Pl. IV.

[14] *B.S.A.*, XIII, 1906/7, Pl. IV; *J.H.S.*, XXXI, 1911, p. 311, Fig. 2; *A.J.A.*, XXXVIII, 1934, Pl. X.

[15] *Bull. Com.*, Dec. 1872-Feb. 1873, pp. 33 ff., Pl. I; Dickins, *J.H.S.*, XXXI, 1911, pp. 308 ff., Fig. 1.

[16] See n. 5 above.

the fish-tail is seen at the back. A distinctive finny collar rests on the shoulders. Other examples in sculpture are a fragment of very high relief in the British Museum,[17] in the style of the giant frieze from Pergamum, on which a headless merman is represented, with numerous drill holes for the insertion of marine appendages in bronze; two torsos in the Vatican and two statues from Pergamum already discussed in connection with Skopas (cf. p. 54).

The merman was rare in the minor arts of the Hellenistic period. On relief vases, as is usual at this time, he is accompanied by a Nereid rider or forms part of a sea thiasos;[18] a Hellenistic lamp from Cyprus has a design in relief of a winged merman;[19] a clay cup from Corinth of the middle of the second century is decorated with an incised design of Poseidon riding in a shell drawn by hippocamps, with a youthful Triton swimming before him (cf. p. 41 and p. 38, n. 13a). In addition, a terracotta of late style, probably found at Tarentum, and now at The Hague, is decorated with a merman and Nereid.[20] These offer nothing new. Distinguished as one of the finest known cameos of the period is a fragment of a sardonyx cameo in the Metropolitan Museum on which a Nereid appears riding a youthful merman.[21] The figures are beautifully modeled with fine muscular detail. The merman resembles some of the figures from the Great Altar at Pergamum. A merman with helmet and lance, usually called Glaukos, because Glaukos was sometimes thought of as a warrior, was used as a coin type at this time in Lucanian Herakleia.[22] The type is the canonical one.

Two-tailed Tritonesses, like other two-tailed marine creatures in Greece, were introduced in the Hellenistic age. Sometimes they were used as supports, *e.g.*, the small female figures found at Lykosura to support the arm of a throne[23] and the figures of mermaids with crossed fish-tails beneath each handle of an egg-shaped relief vase in the British Museum.[23a] A headless torso of the time of the kings, found at Pergamum, was probably used architecturally.[24] The usual type is also found

[17] Smith, *Catalogue of the Greek Sculpture in the British Museum*, London, 1892-1904, III, no. 2220.

[18] See *Appendix*, p. 97.

[19] Metropolitan Museum, no. 2672 (Cesnola Collection).

[20] *Arch. Anz.*, 1922, p. 207, Fig. 6 and p. 211.

[21] Richter, *Catalogue of the Engraved Gems of the Classical Style in the Metropolitan Museum of Art*, New York, 1920, no. 83, Pl. 28.

[22] I.-B. and K., Pl. XI, 20.

[23] *B.S.A.*, XIII, 1906/7, p. 361, Fig. 6.

[23a] *Brit. Mus. Cat. Vases*, IV, G32.

[24] Winter, *Altertümer von Pergamon*, VII, 2, pp. 203 ff., no. 221.

on a Hellenistic relief vase on which a mermaid blowing a conch shell and bearing a vase is ridden by an Eros playing the double flute.[25] It also occurs among the Nereid groups on the wooden sarcophagus mentioned earlier (cf. pp. 52, 72 ff.)[26] and here her feathery girdle spreads out at each side into a kind of wing.

Skylla is not employed on any of the Greek sculptured friezes, but was carved in sculpture in the round. Any connection with Skopas is doubtful, as there is no mention of her in Pliny's description. Without any question, however, there was a famous sculptured group of Skylla seizing the companions of Odysseus[27] and this motif is new. This work has been very imperfectly preserved in fragmentary Roman copies associated with the late Rhodian school. The principal fragment in the Ashmolean Museum at Oxford is part of a torso with a palmette girdle and three dogs' heads attacking human figures that are now much mutilated.[28] Other fragments in various museums appear to be replicas of a youthful and a bearded figure respectively.[29]

By far the majority of the representations of Skylla, however, occur on small monuments such as mirrors and vases. Some of these appear to go back to a prototype of Skylla seizing the companions of Odysseus. It is possible that there was also a painting of this subject. According to ancient writers, Skylla was painted by Androkydes, Phalerion and Nichomachos, of whom we know that only Androkydes surely painted the Homeric Skylla; the others may have painted the daughter of Nisos. Plutarch and Athenaios speak of Androkydes as being from Kyzikos.[30] Athenaios, quoting Polemon, describes the artist as such a great lover of fish that he painted the fish around Skylla with great realism. Of Phalerion we know only that he painted a Skylla.[31] Nichomachos' painting was later set up in Rome in the temple of Peace.[32] For this reason, there is a prevalent opinion that a Roman wall painting from Stabiae

[25] Benndorf, *Griechische und sicilische Vasenbilder*, Berlin, 1869, Pl. LXI, 2; Courby, *op. cit.*, Fig. 70, 24a.

[26] *C.-R.*, 1882/3, Pl. III, 2.

[27] Waser, *op. cit.*, pp. 116 ff.; Klein, *Geschichte der griechische Kunst*, III, Leipzig, 1907, pp. 322 ff. Niketas Choniates describes a bronze group of Skylla in the Hippodrome at Constantinople.

[28] *J.H.S.*, XII, 1891, pp. 52 ff., Figs. 4 and 5 (Farnell).

[29] *Ibid.*, pp. 52 ff., Fig. 3; Amelung, I, *op. cit.*, p. 361, Chiaramonti no. 79, Pl. 38; *Arch. Zeit.*, 1866, pp. 154 ff., Pl. 208; 1870, pp. 57 ff., Pl. 34, 1 and 2 (Schöne).

[30] Plutarch, *Pelop.*, 25; Athenaios, 8, 341a.

[31] Pliny, *N.H.*, XXXV, 143.

[32] *Ibid.*, XXXV, 109.

is a copy of Nichomachos' work.[33] It pictures Skylla snatching the comrades of Odysseus.

Among Hellenistic monuments supposedly showing this style is a handsome mirror from Eretria, in which Furtwängler believed we might see echoes of the art of Nichomachos.[34] Here Skylla is represented with one fish-tail of scaly serpentine character (Fig. 91), huge leafy wings and a leafy girdle, below which appear the foreparts of three animals with crested necks and dragonlike heads. She holds by the hair one of Odysseus' unfortunate companions, while with her other hand she aims at him with an oar. Belonging to the same artistic circle, if not to the same workshop, is a bronze relief of Skylla from Dodona (Fig. 92).[35] There is a strong resemblance in the rendering of the female body and in the engraving of the hair, wings and scales. Neugebauer considered both monuments of Tarentine origin. In the Dodona relief Skylla has two large crested tails symmetrically grouped, a feature uncommon before the Hellenistic period, but one that gradually supplanted the older form and was handed down to Roman art. She carries an oar over her shoulder and was probably slinging a stone with her right hand. Odysseus' adventure is illustrated again on a mirror of similar style from the Crimaea, but here she has but one protome at her girdle.[36] Much of the relief is destroyed, but she is apparently holding a man and attacking him with an oar. The subject recurs on three gems, probably of West Greek workmanship (cf. Fig. 93)[37] and there are additional representations of Skylla on a number of plastic vases and terracottas.[38]

Of the non-human types, the hippocamp is still the most popular as is clear from sculptured friezes and many minor monuments such as jewellery, coins and gems. The Nereid rider is still common, but the old weapon-bearing type is not always used. Often a deity rides in a chariot drawn by hippocamps (cf. p. 74). The winged type persisted in the Hellenistic age mostly in coin types. The new girdle of leafy fins, the curling raised tail, and the smooth body are commonly found.[39]

[33] *Mon. dell'Inst.*, III, 53, 3.

[34] *Arch. Anz.*, 1894, p. 118, Fig. 15; Neugebauer, *Jahrbuch*, XLIX, 1934, pp. 174 ff., Fig. 13; by the same author, *Griechische Bronzen, Meisterwerke in Berlin*, Berlin, 1922, p. 15, Pl. 22. This is in Berlin.

[35] Carapanos, *op. cit.*, Pl. XVIII, 1; Neugebauer, *Jahrbuch*, 1934, pp. 174 ff., Fig. 12 (Athens). [36] *C.-R.*, 1880, Pl. III, 13.

[37] Furtwängler, *A.G.*, Pl. XXXIII, 44-45, 51.

[38] See *Appendix*, pp. 104 ff.

[39] For examples with scales see Reinach, *Stat.*, II, 410, 4; *Brit. Mus. Cat. Vases*, IV, G43.

The span of hippocamps on the large frieze of the Great Altar at Pergamum[40] is one of the most interesting specimens of this motive. The belly line is composed of overlapping rings like a crab's claws and may be actual imitation of this as crab's claws are substituted for tail fins on late monuments. The monster has a crested mane, traces of a continuous spiked fin along the back and an elaborate girdle of overlapping leafy fins.

A hippocamp with a merman driver and a semi-nude Nereid rider is represented on the small frieze from Lamia (Fig. 90).[41] There are many Nereid riders of no especial distinction, such as Doris, the mother of Amphitrite on the frieze of Domitius;[42] in the Vatican the fragmentary early Hellenistic statue which may echo Skopas;[43] and those on two terracotta reliefs from Armento[44] and two on the wooden sarcophagus from the Crimaea.[45] The hippocamp was used not infrequently on Hellenistic vases with plastic designs.[46] A pair painted on a third century askos from Canosa is worthy of note.[47] The figures are painted in white against a pink background. Their spreading wings are done in blue, yellow and two shades of pink.

In the Hellenistic period, as before, the hippocamp is quite commonly a coin type or a symbol, particularly in Italy and Sicily.[48] The types include the hippocamp-rider, who may be Thetis (Fig. 94), Eros, or another divinity; and chariots drawn by hippocamps. The same types were used on gems, though they are more difficult to date (Fig. 95).[49]

Examples of the *ketos* or pistrix, though not numerous in this period, show great diversity of form. A *ketos* with thin, elongated body, perhaps really a sea-serpent, is represented with a Nereid on a Calenian vase.[50] An unusual type which occurs for the first time in the Hellenistic period is best classed with the *ketos*. A small frieze from Pergamum is decorated with figures of Erotes, some of whom ride dolphins; others,

[40] Winnefeld, *op. cit.*, pp. 81 ff., Pl. XX.

[41] See n. 5 above.

[42] See n. 10 above.

[43] Amelung, *op. cit.*, II, p. 158, no. 60A, Pl. 17.

[44] *Abh. d. K. Akad. Wiss. zu Berlin*, 1878, Pl. V, 1-2.

[45] *C.-R.*, 1882/3, Pl. III, 3 and Pl. IV, 6.

[46] See *Appendix*, p. 101.

[47] *Brit. Mus. Cat. Terracottas*, D 185; *C.V.A.*, Brit. Mus., VII, IV Da, Pl. 15, 2b.

[48] See *Appendix*, pp. 101 ff.

[49] See *Appendix*, p. 102.

[50] Pagenstecher, *Die calenische Reliefkeramik*, *Jahrbuch*, *Ergänzungheft*, VIII, 1909, p. 43, no. 39 and Fig. 19.

peculiar creatures with long, snaky necks and the forelegs of a horse.[51] The same monster is represented twice on the wooden sarcophagus from the Crimaea where we are fortunate enough to have the small dragonlike head preserved.[52] Variations of the type also occur on the altar of Domitius.[53] The *ketos* ridden by a Nereid on the Lykosura sculptured drapery (Fig. 88) has a canine head, with horns on the nose, paws like a lion, and a wide girdle of acanthuslike leaves encircling the body.[54] The type common in the fourth century occurs on the wooden sarcophagus and on the frieze of Domitius.[55]

We find for the first time in the Hellenistic period the sea-centaur, -bull, -boar, -stag, -lion, -panther and -pantheress. The sea-lion and sea-stag, well seen on the small frieze from Lamia (Fig. 90), have each a small Eros as rider.[56] One of the Nereids on the altar of Domitius rides a sea-bull.[57] A sea-bull is always the adversary of the small combat frieze from Pergamum (Fig. 85), except in one instance, where we seem to have a sea-boar.[58] A Calenian vase shows a Nereid riding a sea-panther.[59] One of the more curious specimens, found on a Hellenistic gem, is a sea-pantheress attacking a polypus, with a fin or flipper emerging from her right elbow and another from her left shoulder.[60] The Capricorn or sea-goat appears in Greece in the Hellenistic age on a gem in the British Museum.[61] The development of many of these Hellenistic types was carried to a high degree of fantasy in Roman times, as we see from the mosaics in the baths of Ostia (Fig. 102).[62]

[51] Winter, *Altertümer von Pergamon*, VII, 2, pp. 299 ff., no. 386, Pl. XXXIX.
[52] *C.-R.*, 1882/3, Pl. IV, 4 and Pl. V, 15.
[53] See n. 10 above.
[54] See n. 14 above.
[55] *C.-R.*, 1882/3, Pl. III, 6; Pl. IV, 1; Pl. V, 18; see n. 10 above.
[56] See n. 5 above.
[57] See n. 10 above.
[58] See n. 3 above.
[59] Pagenstecher, *op. cit.*, no. 38, Pl. VIII.
[60] Beazley, *The Lewes Collection of Ancient Gems*, Oxford, 1920, p. 86, no. 103; Furtwängler, *A.G.*, Pl. LXI, no. 53.
[61] *British Mus. Cat. Gems*, no. 1205, Pl. XVII. Cf. p. 8, n. 26. Probably of the third century.
[62] Calza, *Ostia*, Rome, 1931, Fig. 13; *The Excavations at Ostia*, Venice, Milan. Rome, Florence, pp. 16 ff.

X

LATE ETRUSCAN SCULPTURE

The monuments to be considered in this chapter belong to the later phase of Etruscan art immediately preceding the Graeco-Roman period. Although the types are largely borrowed from Hellenistic Greek art, the figures are unusual and warrant separate treatment. Unlike Etruscan examples on mirrors and cistae, which for the most part closely resemble Greek models, these Etruscan sea-monsters of late date are practically always changed by the peculiar and sinister Etruscan imagination. Classification is not so easy as heretofore, since some of the types are altered and mixed with others. Skylla, for instance, is replaced by a masculine torso at times. It would seem that the Etruscans often appropriated Greek mythological subjects and modified them to suit their own tastes. The examples to be discussed are mostly from cinerary urns, which are usually of terracotta. There are, however, specimens on sarcophagi and on other reliefs. The principal sites at which these specimens have been found are Chiusi, Perugia and Volterra. The urns have for the most part been studied and classified by Körte.[1]

Late Etruscan reliefs with sea-monsters illustrate the tendency in later Etruscan art to transform Greek types into something wild and unreasonable. What meaning may be attached to these representations is not clear, although most of them seem to be symbolic of the passage of the dead to the other world. Few of our examples appear to have a direct mythological significance. There is no doubt the Etruscans sometimes imagined that the soul was carried to the other world on the back of a sea-monster. Reliefs such as those with representations of Skylla and warriors may refer to adventures of the deceased on his journey to the other world. A relief such as the one from the Tomb of the Reliefs at Cervetri (Fig. 96) which seems to show Skylla with her oar and the dogs at the right may also indicate the dangers confronting the soul on its passage to the West.[2] Certainly the partiality for sea-monsters which we

[1] Körte, *I Relievi delle Urne Etrusche*, III, Berlin, 1916. This is part of a larger work begun by Brunn and carried on by Körte. Many of the urns are illustrated in earlier publications: Gori, *Museum Etruscum*, Florence, 1737- 1743; Conestabile, *De Monumenti di Perugia Etrusca e Romana*, Perugia, 1855-1870; Micali, *Antichi Monumenti*, Florence, 1810.

[2] This is probably the dog of Skylla and not Cerberus. Cf. a stele from Felsina

have already observed in Etruscan tomb paintings and on the stelae from Felsina continued in sepulchral monuments of the latest period.

In addition to the usual examples of the one-tailed merman, old motifs such as riders of *kete*, hippocamps and mermen appear.[3] Besides these, however, are found symbolic figures, such as youthful mermen under the feet of the horses of Pluto's chariot. Here Persephone is being borne to the other world. The merman doubtless typifies the approach to the abode of the dead. The ichthyocentaur, an invention of the Hellenistic age, occurs occasionally on these monuments.[4] The originality of the Etruscan imagination is, however, best seen in specimens which show particularly well their passion for the grotesque. Examples typifying this quality are especially found in reliefs illustrating "Skylla" with the foreparts of sea-gryphons coming from her back, one on each side, which she controls with bridles,[5] or a monster consisting of three female torsos attached to two fish-tails.[6] A masculine version of the same type is also found.[7]

---

where the dogs of Skylla are not attached to her body, Ducati, *Monumenti Antichi*, XX, 1911, pp. 541 ff., Fig. 26 (see Chap. V).

[3] (1) Körte, *op. cit.*, Pl. XXXIII, 10. A merman ridden by a female deity. The monster is youthful and beardless with the acanthus girdle characteristic of Hellenistic Greek sea-monsters. On the monster's tail is an Eros. For another urn, recently excavated at Castiglion del Lago, which is practically identical in design, see *Not. Sc.*, 1934, p. 63, Fig. 4.

(2) *Ibid.*, Pl. XXIX, 3. A merman of the same type carrying a shield and with a suit of armor set up on his back like a trophy.

(3) *Ibid.*, Pl. I and Fig. 1. Persephone being carried to the other world by Pluto. Directly under the horses' feet is a figure of a youthful merman. *Ibid.*, Pl. III, 5 and Fig. 2 is similar but apparently with no mythological significance since the passenger in the chariot is a man. The merman is winged and bearded.

(4) Rumpf, *Staatliche Museen zu Berlin, Katalog der Etruskischen Skulpturen*, Berlin, 1928, E 73 and Pl. 47. Sarcophagus. Cf. Körte, *op. cit.*, p. 31. A relief with a one-tailed merman at each end. Each swims toward the front but turns to look back at a figure of a youth.

One-tailed female deities are rare, but there is one example of such a deity who is represented holding her flying mantle in both hands (Körte, *op. cit.*, Pl. XXIV, 1).

[4] (1) Gori, *op. cit.*, Pl. 149. Urn. An ichthyocentaur carrying a sword and clad in a chlamys which flies out behind.

(2) Körte, *op. cit.*, Pl. XXVIII, 1. The same except that the monster has pectoral fins in place of forelegs.

(3) *Ibid.*, Pl. XXVIII, 2. A sea-centaur carrying off a girl. Cf. *Ibid.*, II, Pl. LXVI where a centaur is carrying off a girl.

[5] *Ibid.*, Pl. XX, 7. Pl. XX, 8 is the same with hippocamps instead of gryphons.

[6] *Ibid.*, Pl. XXVII, 1.

[7] *Ibid.*, Pl. XXVII, 2.

By far the greater number of monsters from the period consist of the two-tailed type of sea-monster, a great many of which have been identified with the Greek Skylla, although the protomai are usually lacking. In most cases the deity is female, but sometimes the masculine character is unquestionable. Almost without exception these Skylla-like figures wear a girdle composed of three acanthus leaves. They are usually winged figures and often a small pair of wings such as are frequently seen on other Etruscan deities are found on the heads. The two long serpentine fish-bodies commonly terminate in leafy tail-fins. One group of reliefs shows the monster in combat with armed warriors. The scene has often been interpreted as Skylla seizing the companions of Odysseus and this is, without doubt, the origin of the motif. Some of these designs bear a striking resemblance to those on the mirrors considered in the last chapter (*see* pp. 76 ff.). A critical examination proves, however, that in most cases the original mythological significance is gone. Only a few examples have the protomai characteristic of the Greek Skylla.[8] It seems probable that the Etruscans associated the combat motif with the trials of the soul after death. Warriors are similarly shown in combat with other monsters, such as gryphons, when there is apparently no direct mythological reference.[9]

A typical example of this combat presents the monster in the middle, with a warrior standing on either side. Often there are two more warriors who have already been caught in the creature's coils. Skylla is fighting with an oar which she holds raised over her shoulder as if ready to strike.[10] A large number of reliefs have representations of the

[8] *Ibid.*, Pl. XI, 1. Also 1a and b. The protomai are lacking in other examples from Perugia. [9] *Ibid.*, Pls. XXXV ff.

[10] For examples with some variations, *see:*

(1) *Ibid.*, Pls. XI, 1-XV, 1; Pryce, *Catalogue of the Sculpture in the British Museum*, I, pt. II, London, 1931, D 50, Fig. 69.

(2) Pryce, *op. cit.*, D 28, Fig. 51. Sarcophagus. At either side is the forepart of a hippocamp.

(3) Körte, *op. cit.*, Pls. XV, 2; XVI, 1, 3. "Skylla" with masculine torso.

(4) *Ibid.*, Pl. XVII, 2. A male "Skylla" holding a young man and young woman in either hand.

(5) *Ibid.*, Pl. XVII, 3. A male fish-tailed deity holding a young girl in his arms. An armed warrior is in one corner.

(6) *Not. Sc.*, 1921, pp. 354 ff., Fig. 6. Pedimental relief, probably from monumental tomb at Vulci. A warrior armed with a shield leaning on the ground beside a fish-tailed monster.

(7) *Mon. dell'Inst.*, III, Pl. 56; Ducati, *Storia dell'Arte Etrusca*, Pl. 170, Fig. 433. Rock Tomb at Sovana. A wingless monster with two fish-tails between two winged demons.

For a discussion of the Etruscan Skylla see Waser, *op. cit.*, pp. 87 ff.

two-tailed monsters alone, usually in the same threatening attitude. The oar is still the most common attribute, but other attributes appear such as a lyre.[11] The goddess is sometimes shown in a symmetrical composition with an anchor in either hand, or she may be throwing a stone like the Greek Skylla (Fig. 97). Ordinarily she is represented without the protomai.[12]

There are also numerous examples of male deities with two fish-tails. Some are of the threatening type; others are more peaceful and bear a closer resemblance to Hellenistic Greek mermen (Fig. 86).[13]

Many urns are decorated with non-human types, such as hippocamps

[11] Körte, *op. cit.*, Pl. XXV, 3.

[12] For examples, *see:*

(1) *Ibid.*, Pls. XVIII, 1; XXI, 2; XXIII, 5; Pryce, *op. cit.*, D 90, Fig. 110; *Arch. Anz.*, 1934, p. 539, Fig. 24; *Not. Sc.*, 1931, p. 488, Fig. 9; Poulsen, *Bildertafeln des Etruskischen Museums der Ny-Carlsberg Glyptothek*, Copenhagen, 1927, Pl. 140, H 308. Skylla with an oar.

(2) Körte, *op. cit.*, Pl. XXII, 3-4; XXIII, 6; Poulsen, *op. cit.*, Pl. 144, H 309. Skylla with anchors.

(3) Körte, *op. cit.*, Pl. XVIII, 2-3; Ducati, *op. cit.*, Pl. 271, Fig. 657 (Fig. 97). Skylla throwing a stone.

(4) Körte, *op. cit.*, Pl. XXV, 4. Skylla with a dagger.

(5) *Ibid.*, p. 37, Fig. 8. Skylla holding a nude baby in her left arm. In her right hand is a fish.

(6) *Ibid.*, Pl. XXI, 1. Skylla without attributes. Cf. Ducati, *op. cit.*, Pl. 177, Fig. 452. Skylla on a capital from Chiusi.

(7) Körte, *op. cit.*, p. 34, Fig. 7. A wingless Skylla with four protomai and two fish-tails ending in dragons' heads. This type is found only on monuments of Puglia. Cf. a relief in the Ingres Collection (*Mon. dell'Inst.*, III, 53, 1) which is almost identical.

[13] For examples, *see:*

(1) Körte, *op. cit.*, Pls. XXI, 7; XXIV, 2; XXV, 5; XXVI, 6; *A.J.A.*, 1918, pp. 252 ff., Figs. 1-2. Male deities with various attributes.

(2) Rumpf, *op. cit.*, E 74, Pl. 49. Stone sarcophagus. A winged male deity with two fish-tails. At either end is a panther ending in a foliate design. Cf. Körte, *op. cit.*, p. 35, XXI, 1c.

(3) Körte, *op. cit.*, p. 39. Cf. Dennis, *Cities and Cemeteries of Etruria*, 3rd ed., London, 1883, I, pp. 473 ff. Stone sarcophagus in the garden of the Casa Campanari. On either side of a krater a male demon with two fish-tails brandishing an oar.

(4) Ducati, *op. cit.*, Pl. 176, Fig. 450. Relief from interior of Tomb of Reliefs at Cervetri (Fig. 96). Skylla?

(5) Körte, *op. cit.*, Pl. XIX, 4-6. Male fish-tailed deities with ears pointed like those of a satyr or Hellenistic Triton.

(6) *Ibid.*, Pl. XXVI, 7. Male deity with two fish-tails. Beneath the girdle two heads which may be dogs' heads are represented in a manner reminiscent of the Greek Skylla (*see* p. 65).

and *kete*. The motif most commonly employed is that of the rider. One group of reliefs shows an armed warrior riding a hippocamp. In another group the monster is ridden by two musicians who vary in the different examples as to costume, sex and the kind of instruments played (Fig. 98). Some hippocamps without riders have wings—a very unusual feature in Etruscan examples. These monsters are all doubtless symbolic in some way of the journey of the deceased to the West.[14]

The *ketos* was freely used by the sculptors of these urns, most often as the steed of a semi-nude goddess (Fig. 99). Usually she rides in a kneeling attitude immediately behind the neck of the monster. Sometimes the rider is a male deity. A relief where the rider is so muffled as to conceal his character probably represents the deceased on his journey to the other world. There are some examples without riders on urns and other monuments (Fig. 100). The monster shows considerable variation in these reliefs. Some *kete* have large heads and thick necks; others small heads on long slender necks. Many are bearded. One monster resembles a goat. One example shows two winged *kete* which would be extraordinary in either Greek or Etruscan art.[15]

[14] For examples, *see:*

(1) *Ibid.*, Pl. XXIX, 1-2. An armed warrior riding a hippocamp.

(2) *Ibid.*, Pl. XXX, 4; p. 42, Fig. 9. Two musicians riding a hippocamp (Fig. 98). For variations, see 4a and b (p. 41).

(3) *Ibid.*, Pl. XXXII, 8-9. Nude youths riding hippocamps.

(4) Pryce, *op. cit.*, D 33, Fig. 55; D 32, Fig. 53; *Mon. dell'Inst.*, VI-VII, Pl. 60 (Martha, *L'art étrusque*, Paris, 1889, Fig. 234; Ducati, *op. cit.*, Pl. 194, Fig. 482). Two hippocamps facing.

(5) Poulsen, *op. cit.*, Pl. 122, H 277. Hippocamp and *ketos* facing.

(6) Körte, *op. cit.*, Pl. CXLIX, 13-14. Winged hippocamps with leafy fin hanging from belly.

(7) *Ibid.*, Pl. CXLIX, 12. Winged horse with fish-tail and leafy fin hanging from belly.

(8) Metropolitan Museum, no. 14.105.8 A-G. Third-century terracotta frieze from Cervetri. Hippocamps and dolphins. There is a similar frieze in Heidelberg.

[15] For examples, *see:*

(1) Körte, *op. cit.*, Pl. XXX, 3. Female deity riding *ketos*. 3a (Fig. 99) is illustrated in Ducati, *op. cit.*, Pl. 276, Fig. 670.

(2) *Ibid.*, Pl. XXXI, 5. Winged female deity riding *ketos*.

(3) *Ibid.*, Pl. XXXIII, 11. A muffled figure riding a *ketos* with goatlike head.

(4) *Ibid.*, Pl. XXXI, 6. Male deity riding *ketos*.

(5) Pryce, *op. cit.*, D 30, Fig. 52 (cast of which D 29 is the cover). Two *kete* with Erotes as riders antithetically grouped about mask. Cf. *Röm. Mitt.*, 1930, p. 177, Fig. 4 where two *kete* are antithetically grouped about a cup.

(6) Körte, *op. cit.*, Pl. LXXVII, 3. Huge bearded *ketos* facing palm tree.

Other animal combinations were not infrequent in Etruria where, as we have seen, new types were at all times readily invented. There are several examples of the sea-panther[16] and the sea-gryphon[17] and one example of the sea-wolf.[18]

On the other side of the tree is a man, probably the deceased, on horseback.

(7) *Ibid.*, Pl. CXLVII, 7; CXLVIII, 8, 10. *Kete.*

(8) *Ibid.*, Pl. CXLVIII, 9; Poulsen, *op. cit.*, Pl. 144, H 310. Winged *kete.*

(9) *Not. Sc.*, 1913, p. 293, Fig. 7; Ducati, *op. cit.*, Pl. 173, Fig. 440. Sima from the pediment of the temple of the Via S. Leonardo, Orvieto. *Ketos* (Fig. 100).

(10) Arndt, *op. cit.*, Pl. 173; *A.J.A.*, XXI, 1917, pp. 298 ff., Fig. 2; Poulsen, *op. cit.*, Pl. 112, H 253. Terracotta grill from Caere. Bearded *ketos.*

[16] For examples, *see:*

(1) Körte, *op. cit.*, Pl. XXXI, 7. Nude boy riding backwards on sea-panther.

(2) Conestabile, *op. cit.*, Pl. XXXVIII-LXIII. Two sea-panthers used decoratively. The monsters have wings which continue around the neck in a leafy collar and a foliate tail-fin.

(3) Rumpf, *op. cit.*, E 74, Pl. 49 (cf. above, n. 13, no. 2). Above the relief of the fish-tailed deity a frieze of sea-panthers.

[17] For examples, *see:*

(1) Brunn, *I Relievi delle Urne Etrusche*, Rome, 1870, Pl. XXXVI, 3. Two sea-gryphons facing in a pedimental composition.

(2) Körte, *op. cit.*, Pl. XX, 7 (cf. above, n. 5). Skylla with two sea-gryphons projecting from her back.

(3) Körte, *op. cit.*, Pl. XLIII. Fury with the foreparts of sea-gryphons projecting from her back.

[18] *Ibid.*, Pl. CXLIX, 11. Winged sea-wolf.

XI

THE YOUTHFUL DOLPHIN-RIDER

The youthful dolphin-rider, though not a sea-monster, is distinctly related to some of the representations of a deity riding a sea-monster and deserves mention in this connection. There are several stories in Greek mythology which are concerned with the rescue of a youthful hero by a dolphin. The most famous of these have to do with Arion and Melikertes-Palaimon of Corinth and with Taras and Phalanthos of Tarentum. Less well-known are Enalos of Lesbos and Eikadios, who according to one tradition was a Cretan and a brother of Iapyx, the eponymous hero of Iapygia.[1] In this connection one should recall the story told in the Homeric hymn to Pythian Apollo, where Apollo in the guise of a dolphin guided some Cretan sailors to Delphi to be his ministers.[2] Perhaps all these dolphin stories should be connected with Crete.

The story of Arion is almost too well-known to need repetition. The oldest extant version of the tale is found in Herodotus, although the story seems to have been told also by Hellanikos.[3] Arion, a native of Methymna in Lesbos, was a noted poet and performer on the lyre, who spent most of his life at the court of the tyrant Periander in Corinth. After a visit to Sicily and Italy he took ship for Corinth from Tarentum. During the voyage the sailors robbed him and threatened his life, so that he was forced to jump overboard. A dolphin, however, came to his rescue and carried him on its back safely to Taenaron, whence he made his way back to Corinth. At Taenaron was a statue of Arion with his lyre sitting on the back of a dolphin.[4] How did Arion who lived at the end of the seventh century, become attached to this legend? There must be some underlying myth of a favorite hero saved by a dolphin.

The story of Melikertes-Palaimon is closely linked with that of his mother Ino-Leukothea. Ino was a daughter of Kadmos and a sister of Semele, the mother of Dionysos. She incurred the anger of her husband, Athamas, by suckling the infant Dionysos after the death of his mother. After Athamas had killed their son, Learchos, she fled with her other son, Melikertes. They jumped into the sea near Megara and became

[1] Servius on *Aeneid*, III, 332 (after Cornificius Longus).

[2] *Pythian Apollo*, 388 ff.

[3] Herodotus, I, 23 ff.

[4] Herodotus, I, 24; Pausanias, III, 25, 7.

marine deities under the names of Leukothea and Palaimon. The body of Melikertes was brought ashore near Corinth by a dolphin.[5] On the way from Corinth to Lechaion was a statue of Palaimon on a dolphin, together with Leukothea and Poseidon.[6] The Isthmian games were founded in honor of Palaimon.

Melikertes has been commonly connected with the Phoenician god Melqart, but this theory has of late been somewhat discredited. Indeed, there seems to be little to recommend it beyond a chance resemblance of names. Melikertes is represented as a youth, Melqart as a mature man with a beard. Nor is any female deity associated with Melqart. Leukothea and Palaimon are Greek names and their meaning is clear. Ino and Melikertes are not certainly Greek and their meaning is unknown.[7] Farnell sees much that may be Cretan in the cult of Ino and Melikertes, particularly the mother-goddess associated with a youthful male god.[8] The leap of Ino resembles the ritual leap of Britomartis. If this is correct, we may perhaps believe also that the connection of the dolphin with Melikertes goes back to Crete.

Enalos of Lesbos jumped into the sea to save his beloved who was being sacrificed to Amphitrite and the Nereids. Or, according to another tradition, he jumped into the sea with her believing her rescue impossible. Both were brought safely to land by a dolphin. This legend is connected with the founding of Lesbos. In one version the girl is the daughter of Phineus;[9] in another the daughter of Smintheus, one of the seven founders of Lesbos who landed on *μεσόγειον ἕρμα* under the leadership of Echalos and there offered a virgin to Amphitrite and the Nereids and a bull to Poseidon.[10] The name Smintheus at once suggests a pre-Greek divinity and recalls the cult of Apollo Smintheus. We have inscriptional evidence that this cult existed at Methymna in Imperial times.[11] One scholar, at least, believes that the Smintheion was at Arisba, a town whose inhabitants were early reduced to slavery by the people of Methymna.[12] It is generally accepted that the name Smintheus is de-

[5] Pausanias, I, 44, 8; Lucian, *Dial. Mar.*, 8, 1; Philostratus, *Imag.*, II, 16.

[6] Pausanias, II, 3, 4. Cf. also *ibid.*, II, 1, 8 and II, 2, 1.

[7] See Introduction. Maass, *Griechen und Semiten auf dem Isthmus von Korinth*, Berlin, 1903, pp. 12 ff., derives Melikertes from μέλι "honey" and κείρω "to cut". The name is thus purely Greek and means "honey-cutter". Cf. Wilamowitz, *op. cit.*, I, p. 218, n. 1.

[8] Farnell, *Greek Hero Cults*, Oxford, 1921, pp. 45 ff.

[9] Plutarch, *de Soll. Anim.*, Chap. 36 (*Frm. Hist. Gr.*, IV, p. 459) after Myrsilos of Lesbos.

[10] Plutarch, *Sept. Sapient. Conviv.*, Chap. 20.

[11] *C.I.G.*, 21906.

[12] Tümpel, *Philologus*, XLIX, 1890, pp. 89 ff. Cf. Herodotus, I, 151.

rived from the pre-Greek word for "mouse" and that the origin of the cult is Lycian. There was probably, then, pre-Greek influence in Lesbos in the pre-Aeolic period. The dolphin legend probably also belongs to an earlier time. It should be noted that Arion came originally from Lesbos.

Eikadios was an epithet of Apollo at certain places where a festival was held in his honor on the twentieth day of the month. Out of this must have grown the legend of the hero Eikadios. In the list of Arkadian kings, he was the son of Doricus and Koronea, that is of Apollo and Korone. In Patara, the city of Apollo Patareus, he was the son of Apollo and a local nymph, Lycia.[13] The Lycians regarded him as the founder of Delphi, the true Apollo Delphinios. When he was about to sail to Italy, he was shipwrecked and carried on a dolphin to Delphi. Cornificius Longus makes him a Cretan and the brother of Iapyx.[14] He was carried on a dolphin to Delphi while Iapyx went to Italy. He named Delphi from the dolphin, and the low-lying fields he called Crisaeus or Cretaeos from his native land. This last legend tends to show that tradition connected Apollo Delphinios with Crete.

The dolphin is associated with two Tarentine heroes, Taras and Phalanthos. Taras was the eponymous hero who gave his name to the city and the river. There are various traditions about him. According to Pausanias, he was the son of Poseidon and a local nymph.[15] The founding of the city was usually ascribed to Phalanthos who brought the Parthenians from Sparta, but one authority gives Taras as the founder of the city which Phalanthos enlarged.[16] There is also a tradition that he was a descendant of Herakles and came to Tarentum from Sparta. In another story Taras had a son by Satyria, daughter of Minos.This son was shipwrecked and carried to Italy on the back of a dolphin.[17] There seems to be some authority, however, for Satyria being the mother of Taras himself. This would make him a grandson of Minos of Crete.

There are even more different versions of the birth of Phalanthos. He is described as a Spartan, an Amyklaian, a Heraklid, a son of Poseidon and finally a son of Aratus.[18] He is best known as the leader of the Parthenians who left Sparta after the first Messenian War to settle in

[13] Servius on *Aeneid*, III, 332.

[14] Cf. n. 1 above.

[15] Pausanias, X, 10, 8.

[16] Servius on *Aeneid*, III, 551.

[17] Probus on *Georg.*, II, 197.

[18] Spartan: Pausanias, X, 10, 3; Amyklaian: Silius Italicus, VII, 665; Laconian: Horace, *Carm.*, II, 6, 11; Heraklid: Servius on *Georg.*, IV, 125; son of Poseidon: Acro on Horace, *Carm.*, I, 28, 29; son of Aratus: Justin, III, 4, 8.

Tarentum.[19] The story can be traced back as far as Antiochos of Syracuse. Pausanias tells of his shipwreck in the Crisaian bay and of his rescue by a dolphin.[20] Phalanthos and Taras are mentioned together in Pausanias' description of the Tarentine dedication by Onatas at Delphi. Near Phalanthos was a representation of a dolphin.[21] There were two other Phalanthoi, one at home in Arcadia and Achaea and the other at home in Rhodes. Studniczka believed that Phalanthos was a pre-Dorian, Peloponnesian aspect of Poseidon and that he belonged in Arcadia and Achaea. His cult spread to Italy before the Spartan colonization of Tarentum, but was too strong to be suppressed.[22] Phalanthos, however, has the characteristic νθ of pre-Greek names such as Smintheus and Hyakinthos. It seems quite possible that the name is pre-Greek and that the cult of the dolphin may go back to Crete, for there is additional evidence of the Cretans in Southern Italy.

There is, in fact, a strong tradition that Minos pursued Daidalos to Sicily and was treacherously slain there at the palace of King Kokalos of Kamikos.[23] The oldest and most complete version of the story is found in Herodotus. All the Cretans but the Polichnitians and Praesians went to Sicily to avenge the death of their king, but not being able to take Kamikos after a siege of five years they sailed for home. They were shipwrecked, however, off the coast of Southern Italy where they settled and became the Messapian Iapygians. Athenaios' description of the Iapygians fits the Minoans.[24] He mentions their painted faces, their flowered robes and the magnificence of their houses as compared with their shrines. According to one legend, Iapyx, the eponymous hero of Iapygia, was the son of Daidalos and a Cretan woman who came to Sicily with Minos.[25] In another story already mentioned he was a Cretan and a brother of Eikadios.[26]

Strabo speaks of a tradition that the Salentini were Cretans.[27] There were also current in ancient times stories of Cretans having settled at Brundisium, but the general belief was that they did not stay there.[28]

Among the cults of Tarentum was that of Zeus Kataibates, who de-

[19] Strabo, VI, 278 ff.
[20] Pausanias, X, 13, 10.
[21] Pausanias, X, 13, 10.
[22] Studniczka, *Kyrene*, Leipzig, 1890, pp. 192 ff.
[23] Herodotus, VII, 170; Pausanias, VII, 4, 5-6; Strabo, VI, 272.
[24] Atheniaios, XII, 522 ff.
[25] Strabo, VI, 279; Pliny, *N.H.*, III, 11, 16.
[26] Servius on *Aeneid*, III, 332 and XI, 247.
[27] Strabo, VI, 281.
[28] Strabo, VI, 282.

scended in thunder. Klearchos, a pupil of Aristotle, states that the Tarentines having overthrown Karbina, a city of the Iapygians, and having outraged the inhabitants, were punished by being struck by lightning. The Tarentines erected pillars in front of their doors corresponding to the number of men who failed to return. These were still in front of the houses in the time of the writer and the Tarentines instead of lamenting the dead offered sacrifices to Zeus Kataibates. Death by lightning was here regarded as an honor.[29] The Tarentines called the god Zeus Kataibates, but this form of his worship was not known in other places where the cult was practised.[30] The pillar cult points toward Crete where the pillar played an important part in religious ceremonies. Cook believes that the Pythagorean or quasi-Pythagorean cult of the sky-pillar which originated in Southern Italy may have had Cretan antecedents.[31] He also wishes to derive the thunderbolts of Zeus from the double axe, but this theory is not universally accepted and seems, on the whole, doubtful.[32]

Pre-Greek elements have been recognized in the cult of the Dioscuri, which is supposed to have come to Tarentum from Sparta.[33] Peculiar symbols connected with their worship at Tarentum, such as two amphorae on votive terracottas may go back to the Cretan period. Polybios speaks of a grave mound called by some that of Hyakinthos, by others that of Apollo Hyakinthos.[34] It seems clear that Hyakinthos was a pre-Greek deity, identified later with Apollo. It is possible, therefore, that the cult of Hyakinthos at Tarentum goes back to the Cretan settlement, although it might also have come to Tarentum from Sparta.

After examining the different legends connected with the dolphin-rider, it seems probable that they go back to a single dolphin-god who was at home in Crete or came to the mainland from Lycia *via* Crete. At an early period in Greek history the dolphin-god was identified with Apollo. There is a good deal of evidence to show that the cult of Apollo Delphinios started in Crete and spread north.[35] There are traces of it in Crete, particularly at Knossos.[36]

The dolphin-rider is represented on ancient monuments of the

[29] Athenaios, XII, 522E-523B.

[30] Cook, *Zeus*, Cambridge, 1914-1925, II, pp. 29 ff.

[31] *Ibid.*, II, p. 45.

[32] Farnell, "Cretan Influence in Greek Religion", *Essays in Aegaean Archaeology*, edited by Casson, Oxford, 1927, pp. 9 ff.

[33] Nilsson, *op. cit.*, p. 470.

[34] VIII, 30.

[35] Vs. this view, cf. Wilamowitz, *op. cit.*, I, p. 145, n. 2.

[36] Farnell, *Cults of the Greek States*, IV, Oxford, 1907, pp. 145 ff.

archaic period as well as later. Unfortunately we know very little about the statues of men on dolphins mentioned in literature. The most famous of these was the statue of Arion at Taenaron, but Melikertes-Palaimon was so represented at Corinth and Taras or Phalanthos at Tarentum.[37]

A youthful dolphin-rider, almost certainly Melikertes-Palaimon, forms the decoration of some of the Corinthian pinakes.[38] The figure is practically identical with the young god shown riding a sea-monster on some of the pinakes already discussed (*see* p. 29 and Fig. 41). The same design is used on one of the Graeco-Phoenician gems from Sardinia (Fig. 15e).[39] The figure is a beardless youth very similar to the hippocamp-rider represented on another gem (cf. Fig. 15a). Two youthful dolphin-riders are represented on a black-figured lekythos from Gela, now in the collection of Professor D. M. Robinson.[39a] A satyr kneeling on a high rock in the middle of the sea pours wine from an oenochoe into a phiale held by a youth who rides a dolphin. Behind the satyr is another youth riding away on a dolphin. These young riders surely have no connection with the bearded Melqart who is shown riding a sickle-winged hippocamp on late fifth- and fourth-century Tyrian coins (Fig. 37b).[40]

The dolphin-rider was the most characteristic coin type of Tarentum from the very beginning (Fig. 101).[41] There has been some difference of opinion as to whether the rider is Phalanthos or Taras. Studniczka has advanced good reasons for believing that Phalanthos is represented.[42] In the first place, the inscription τάρας which appears on the coins is used on other Tarentine coins with different deities and so must refer to the city and not to the god. In the second place, the same coin type appears later at Brundisium, a city which was hostile to Tarentum and which therefore would not have adopted a Tarentine river-god. Phalanthos, however, was associated with Brundisium and would have been entirely appropriate. Aristotle tells us, however, that in his time the

[37] Arion: see n. 4 above; Melikertes-Palaimon: see n. 6 above; Taras or Phalanthos: Probus on *Georg.*, II, 197.

[38] Pernice, *op. cit.*, F470. Melikertes lying on the back of a dolphin was a very common reverse type on Corinthian coins of the Roman Imperial period (*Brit. Mus. Cat. Coins, Corinth*, pp. 67, 75, 78, 80, 82, 85; Pls. XVII, 5; XIX, 14; XX, 12, 21, 22; XXI, 12).

[39] Furtwängler, *A.G.*, Pl. XV, no. 39.

[39a] *C.V.A.*, U.S., IV, Robinson Collection, Pl. 37, 3a-c.

[40] See Chap. IV, n. 29.

[41] Evans, "The Horseman of Tarentum", *Numismatic Chronicle*, 1889, Pl. I, 1; Head, *op. cit.*, pp. 52 ff.

[42] Studniczka, *op. cit.*, pp. 175 ff.

dolphin-rider was believed to be Taras, the son of Poseidon.[43] According to another view, Taras was later substituted for Phalanthos.

The earliest Tarentine coins with the dolphin-rider are of the incuse variety. The deity is represented completely nude and is shown in a stiff archaic pose. He has no attributes. Usually one arm is outstretched and the other rests on the dolphin's back, but sometimes both are outstretched. Evans dates these coins as early as 560 B.C., but others put them in the second half of the sixth century. The second group has a four-spoked wheel as a reverse type and uses the dolphin-rider as the obverse type. The wheel was soon replaced by a hippocamp with sickle wings.[44] Not much later the larger denominations have as a reverse type a male head, perhaps Taras, or a female head, usually called Satyria. On all these coins, the dolphin-rider retains the archaic scheme of the incuse coins.

The dolphin-rider continued to be used as a coin type at Tarentum down through the period of Hannibalic occupation. The type is also found at Valetium and Brundisium.[45]

[43] Aristotle, Frm. 590.

[44] Evans, *op. cit.*, p. 2.

[45] For additional information on the dolphin-rider see Usener, *Sintflutsagen*, Bonn, 1899 and Stebbins, *The Dolphin in the Literature and Art of Greece and Rome*, Baltimore, 1929, p. 116.

CONCLUSION

This study has attempted to trace the origin and evolution of the types of sea-monsters employed on the monuments of Greece and Etruria. It remains to state briefly the conclusions drawn from such a study.

By means of numerous examples we have given weight to the generally accepted theory that the merman as an artistic type originated in the Orient. Recent excavations show that this type probably existed as early as 3000 B.C. (*see* Chap. I). There is every reason to assume that the merman was borrowed by the Greeks from the East, for it first appears on Greek monuments of the Orientalizing period. Examples in this period are most common in sites closely in touch with the Orient, such as Ionia, Corinth, Attica and Etruria.

The Greeks adopted the merman type in the Orientalizing period for representations of Halios Geron, who was almost certainly the principal pre-Greek sea-deity and hence the predecessor of Poseidon. He survived, however, as a minor sea-god. The separate existence of a nameless Old Man of the Sea seems clearly established although several other minor sea-divinities had the name Halios Geron as a secondary title. Nereus, Proteus, Triton, Phorkys and Glaukos are all quite distinct, but have something in common, which caused them to be identified with Halios Geron. Associated with the Old Man of the Sea was a group of sea-maidens, his daughters. After the identification of Nereus and Halios Geron, the maidens were known as Nereids. In a very early legend a Greek hero fought with and conquered the Old Man of the Sea. A hero, usually recognizable as Herakles, is shown wrestling with a fish-tailed monster on many archaic monuments (Figs. 10, 14, 24, 25, 27, 28). It seems probable that this design was also borrowed from Oriental art where contests of men and monsters are common (*see* Chap. II, n. 16).

The merman had a continuous evolution in Greek art. The motive of Herakles wrestling with a sea-monster disappears after the archaic period. In the fifth century the type becomes greatly humanized; Triton is no longer δεινὸς θεός, as in Hesiod. He is usually represented clothed and appears as an aide of Poseidon or as the friend and playmate of the Nereids. The Hellenistic age brings a decided change when the merman is often shown with a Nereid on his back. He now becomes part of a sea thiasos comparable to the Bacchic thiasoi and may be represented any number of times on the same monument. The relation of the merman to the Nereids is often of an erotic character. Animal ears sometimes further suggest his likeness to Bacchic creatures such as satyrs and centaurs. Rather bizarre variations of the merman type are introduced in the Hellenistic period such as the two-tailed "Triton", the ichthyocentaur, etc.

The Tritoness or mermaid type probably existed in the Orient, although there is no definite monumental evidence (*see* p. 7). Evidence for the worship of a female fish-tailed deity in Syria, though late, is fairly conclusive. The mermaid type was never common in Greek art, but appears occasionally from the archaic period onward.

Skylla occurs for the first time on monuments of the fifth century where she is represented as a much humanized mermaid with the foreparts of dogs joined to her body (Figs. 66, 67). This type is clearly an invention of fifth-century Greek artists and has no very close connection with the Skylla described in Homer. The legend of Skylla is doubtless very old and may have come originally from Phoenicia (*see* p. 43). It is possible that it came to Greece through the Minoans, who as a seafaring people, would certainly have had legends of sea-monsters. Skylla was particularly common on monuments of Sicily and Southern Italy, where she appears on many coins (Fig. 68). Monuments of the Hellenistic age often show Skylla seizing the companions of Odysseus (Fig. 93). Fragments of sculpture prove that there was a famous sculptured group of this period representing the subject. The same theme may have also been illustrated in a painting.

The dolphin-rider types, both male and female, are interesting in connection with the fish-tailed types. The male dolphin-rider has been derived from the Orient by those who believe that Melikertes is a form of Melqart. The principal legends of the boy and the dolphin can nearly all be found to have Cretan connections. In the story of Melikertes there are traces of the Minoan mother and child cult and the ritual leap. It seems probable that the Tarentine dolphin-rider, Taras-Phalanthos, is Cretan, especially since we have evidence of early connections between Southern Italy and Crete. The idea that the merman and dolphin-rider may be different conceptions of the same deity seems improbable.[1] The dolphin-rider is always represented as a young boy. The archaic merman, on the other hand, is a bearded old man.

The female dolphin-rider or Nereid appears early in Greek art, but there seems to be no reason for believing that the type had any real connection with the male rider. The motif seems to be purely Greek

[1] Keller, *Thiere des classischen Altertums*, Innsbruck, 1887, pp. 214 ff. Aly, *Philologus*, LXVIII, 1909, p. 430.

and is probably older than the variations with the hippocamp and *ketos*. The Nereid is often shown carrying the armor of Achilles. Abundant monumental evidence proves that the type is much older than Skopas, who was formerly credited with its invention (*see* Chap. IV).

The hippocamp or sea-horse is doubtless of Oriental origin. Although all the evidence points to the Orient, there are no monuments to help us. In the archaic period the hippocamp appears often on Island gems and on the animal friezes of Ionic and Etruscan monuments, whose Eastern connections are clear. He was also particularly common on Etruscan sepulchral monuments, where he must have had some significance in connection with the journey to the West. The figure often associated with the hippocamp in Greek art, the Nereid rider, occurs frequently from the fifth century onward. In the Hellenistic age hippocamps are often represented with Nereid riders in sea thiasoi. The design of a chariot drawn by hippocamps first becomes common in the Hellenistic age, although invented earlier.

Although the *ketos* or pistrix may have Oriental forebears, it seems problable that the type came to Greece by way of Crete (*see* pp. 28 ff., Fig. 39). The sea-creature pictured on the Minoan seal impression has the essential characteristics of the Greek *ketos*, the canine head, large, erect ears and open jaw. On an early Corinthian vase illustrating the story of Perseus and Andromeda (Fig. 38) the monster, which is labeled "ketos" is very similar. Like the hippocamp, the *ketos* is most often associated with the Nereid rider. In the Hellenistic age a fantastic variation of the *ketos* with long snaky tail appears for the first time.

The most famous single monument of antiquity on which sea-monsters were represented was of course Skopas' famous group. This unfortunately does not survive, nor are there any statues which are definitely known to be copies of any part of it. The closest is probably the Nereid found at Ostia (Fig. 71). Certain statues of mermen, though much later, seem to reflect the art of Skopas (Fig. 72). Perhaps Skopas was responsible for some of the new types which appear in the Hellenistic period.

The Hellenistic age was indeed an age of innovation. Many new and fantastic types of sea-monsters were introduced and the sea thiasos was very popular. Interpretation of the monuments is extremely difficult. It is probable that in some cases, at least, the journey of the deceased is indicated. On a grave stele from the Peiraeus the two mermen are clearly symbolic (Fig. 87).

Of great interest are the fish-tailed monsters represented on Etruscan monuments of all periods. In general we find the Etruscans copying

Greek models. Sometimes, as on the Praenestine cistae, the copying is quite faithful, but more often they introduce features which give their monuments their peculiarly Etruscan character. There is a good deal of invention at all times, for certain combinations like the deity with fins on his garments (Fig. 46) and the fish-tailed Pegasus (*see* p. 83, n. 14, no. 7) they had surely never seen in any other art. Interpretation is difficult, but it seems fairly certain that many of the monsters represented on sepulchral monuments are symbolic figures of some sort. The Etruscans apparently believed that the next world was reached by a sea-voyage. The hippocamp and, on later monuments, also the *ketos*, very probably were supposed to convey the deceased to his new abode. "Skylla" and the warriors may represent the trials of the soul after death. It is clear that the other world is sometimes typified by a sea-monster (*see* Chap. X).

It is interesting to consider what the various sea-monsters meant to the Greeks and to the artists who created them. The early dangers of navigation undoubtedly gave rise to the idea of the Old Man of the Sea who wrestled with heroes and gods. He was the personification of the treachery of the constantly changing sea and these changes gave rise to the idea of his metamorphoses. In more friendly mood, he must often have been credited with pointing the way to the sailor and so we have the story telling how he prophesied to Menelaos and others on their journeys. Under one of his aspects, Palaimon, he was adored as a sea-god friendly to the shipwrecked.[2] He belonged to the Orient and early Mediterranean world and was called by various names before Poseidon usurped his authority. By the fifth century his dread aspects had largely disappeared and he became a comrade of the Nereids and other sea-creatures. In the Hellenistic age his importance was still further lessened and he is usually seen as part of a sea thiasos along with other sea-monsters, who were always subordinate in their significance.

The mermaid and the siren-fish were doubtless malevolent in early times, perhaps personifications of a destructive power luring men to their dooms. Skylla may be a glorification of this type, but her domain was limited to the rocky coasts of the Mediterranean.

After the Old Man of the Sea, Skylla is perhaps the most vivid marine personality. She seems to have personified a dangerous rocky coast in the beginning. The early types show her as ἀποσκοπῶν, shading her eyes with her hands, looking out over the waves. In later times she may have

[2] Vergil, *Georg.*, I, 437; *Aeneid*, V, 823; Euripides, *Iph. in Tau.*, 271.

been merely a symbol of the sea or even of a sea-victory (cf. Thurium, p. 60 and p. 60, n. 55).

The hippocamp may have been derived from the sea-horse, common in the Orient and in Mediterranean waters. The presence in the epic of Aleiyan Ba'al of Kousor urging that the elements be unreined against Ba'al indicates that we have here the literary prototype for the hippocamps on Phoenician coins.[3] His route to Greece is thus traced from the Orient *via* Phoenicia to Crete and Melos and to Southern Italy *via* Sicily and Tarentum. In Greece he is a personification, in all probability of the waves of the sea and their swiftness. He was always a minor denizen of the ocean in Greece, where he does not seem to have been a god and where he appears to have none of the terrorizing aspects associated with the *ketos*. He is usually employed as a decorative figure and may often merely have personified the sea, especially in late times. His presence on the coins of Sybrita and on the bronze state seal of Larissa Kremaste, inland sites, may have indicated that the commerce of these places extended to the sea.

The most sinister of marine monsters after Skylla is the *ketos*, dog-headed to symbolize the barking of the waves, and evidently given to preying upon ships, if we are to trust the Minoan prototype. By the fifth century he is tamed and ridden by the Nereids. Like the dolphin-rider he survives into the fourth century A.D., as we see from the Roman mosaics at Antioch (Fig. 103).[4]

[3] See Chap. I, n. 31.

[4] Cambell, *A.J.A.*, XL, 1936, p. 4 and Fig. 6.

APPENDIX

I. *THE MERMAN*

A. ETRUSCAN RED WARE FROM CAERE

1. Micali, *Monumenti Inediti*, Florence, 1844, Pl. XXXIV, 3.
2. Pottier, *Vases Antiques du Louvre*, I, Pl. 38, D340, 341, 342. Also *Louvre*, D308 and 343.
3. *Berlin*, no. 1639.
4. Masner, *Die Sammlung Antiker Vasen und Terracotten in K. K. Oesterreich. Museum*, Vienna, 1892, no. 209.
5. *C.V.A.*, University of Michigan, I, U.S., III, Pl. XXII, Fig. 5. Just a fish-tail is preserved which may belong either to a hippocamp or a merman.

B. HELLENISTIC RELIEF VASES

1. Courby, *op. cit.*, Fig. 70, 24b; Dumont-Chaplain, *Les céramiques de la Grèce propre*, Paris, 1888, Pl. XXXIII, 5. Megarian bowl. Merman with hippocamp and Eros.
2. Graef, *op. cit.*, II, no. 1260, Pl. 90. Megarian bowl. Merman with hippocamps and Erotes.
3. *Archaeologia*, XVII, Pl. X; *Brit. Mus. Cat.*, IV, G 102. Megarian bowl. Merman with Eros on his back, four times repeated.
4. *Brit. Mus. Cat.*, IV, G 20. Plastic lekythos from Ruvo. Merman clad in pink chiton and holding Nereid.
5. Pagenstecher, *op. cit.*, no. 36, Fig. 18; Benndorf, *op. cit.*, Pl. LVII, 4; *Brit. Mus. Cat.*, IV, G 127. Calenian phiale. Youthful merman with Nereid.

II. *THE HIPPOCAMP*

A. ATTIC BLACK-FIGURED VASES SHOWING OLD MAN ON HIPPOCAMP

1. *Brit. Mus. Cat. Vases*, II, B428, *C.V.A.*, Brit. Mus., III, III He, Pl. 20, 1b. Also Gerhard, *op. cit.*, Pl. 8; Lenormant-de Witte, *Élite céramographique*, Paris, 1844-1457, III, Pl. I; Reinach, *Repertoire des vases peints*, 2nd ed., Paris, 1922, II, p. 22. Eye cylix with design of hippocamp on either side between eyes. The monster is wingless (Fig. 36).

2. *Berlin*, no. 2063. Cylix with similar design. The monster is wingless.
3. Pottier, *Catalogue des vases peints*, F 145; *Cataloghi del Museo Campana*, Rome, 1860?, Cl. IV, no. 751; deWitte, *Notice sur les vases peints du Musée Napoléon*, III, Paris, 1862, p. 21. The design is similar, but in the interior.
4. *Hermitage*, no. 11. Lekythos with similar design. The monster is winged.
5. Jahn, *Beschreibung der Vasensammlung König Ludwigs in der Pinakothek zu München*, Munich, 1854, no. 361. Lekythos with similar design. The monster is winged.
6. P. Gardner, *Catalogue of the Vases in the Ashmolean Museum*, Oxford, 1893, p. 17, no. 247. Lekythos with similar design. The monster is winged.
7. Metropolitan Museum, no. 17.230.9. Skyphos with similar design. The monster is winged.
8. Christie, *Disquisitions upon the Painted Greek Vases, etc.*, London, 1825, p. 10. An illustration from such a vase stands at the top of the page, but the shape of the vase is not known. The monster is winged.
9. Amphora in Strassburg. von Wahl, *op. cit.*, p. 14, no. 19.

B. ETRUSCAN RED WARE FROM CAERE

1. Pottier, *Vases antiques du Louvre*, Pl. 38, D340, 341, and 342. Also *Louvre*, D308 and 343.
2. Mingazzini, *Vasi della Collezione Castellani, Catalogo*, Rome, 1930, no. 281 (Pls. XII, 4 and XIV, 2, 3) and no. 284 (Pl. XIII, 5).
3. *Berlin*, nos. 1639 and 1640.
4. Blümner, *Die Archaeologische Sammlung in Eidgenössischen Polytechnikum zu Zürich*, Zurich, 1881, B48 (p. 182).

C. RED-FIGURED VASES FROM SOUTH RUSSIA

1. *Hermitage*, no. 1915. *C.-R.*, 1866, Pl. III; Overbeck, *op. cit.*, Atlas, V, 120, a and b. Two Nereids riding hippocamps.
2. *C.-R.*, 1880, p. 106. Thiasos with a merman and a Nereid on a hippocamp.
3. *C.-R.*, 1876, Pl. V. Fragments of fish plates. Four examples of Nereids on hippocamps (nos. 10-13) and one of merman (14).

4. *Hermitage*, no. 1799. Thiasos with a Nereid on a hippocamp and a merman. Cf. *C.-R.*, 1866, p. 81.
5. *Hermitage*, no. 1800. Thiasos with a Nereid on a hippocamp and a Tritoness. Cf. *C.-R.*, 1866, p. 82.

D. SOUTH ITALIAN VASES

(Examples not mentioned in text)

1. *Brit. Mus. Cat. Vases*, IV, F 69; Inghirami, *Galleria Omerica*, II, Pl. 166. Nereids riding sea-animals and carrying armor. A Nereid with a shield, probably Thetis, is riding a hippocamp.
2. *Jatta Collection*, no. 1496; *Mon. dell'Inst.*, III, Pl. XX, Heydemann, *op. cit.*, Pl. V, 1. Handleless krater from Ruvo. Nereids riding sea-animals and carrying armor. The hippocamp has a scaly body.
3. *Jatta Collection*, no. 1500; Heydemann, *op. cit.*, Pl. IV; Roscher's *Lexikon*, s.v. "Nereiden," Figs. 4 and 5. South Italian amphora of late style. Nereids riding sea-animals and carrying armor.
4. *Jatta Collection*, no. 425; Heydemann, *op. cit.*, Pls. I-II. Large amphora from Ruvo. Nereids riding sea-animals and carrying armor.
5. Louvre. Inghirami, *Galleria Omerica*, II, Pl. 170. Nereid riding hippocamp with scaly body and carrying armor.
6. *Naples*, no. 3252. Cf. p. 89, n. 30, and Beazley, *J.H.S.*, XLVII, 1927, p. 228, n. 25. Style late and poor. On neck, winged hippocamp. In lower row, Nereid on hippocamp carrying shield and trident.
7. *Berlin*, no. 3241; Gerhard, *Apulische Vasen*, Berlin, 1845, Pl. VII. Europa on the bull accompanied by a Nereid on a hippocamp.
8. *Berlin*, no. 3258; Gerhard, *op. cit.*, Pl. X. On foot of vase, Nereid riding hippocamp.
9. *Berlin*, nos. 3608-3610. Fish plates of uncertain Italian fabric. Hippocamps with other sea-animals.
10. *Annali*, 1857, Pl. G. Apulian askos formerly in Collection Avellino in Naples. Present whereabouts unknown. Hippocamps. Cf. *Brit. Mus. Cat. Terracottas*, D 203, Fig. 69.

E. CISTAE FROM PRAENESTE

1. *Brit. Mus. Cat. Bronzes*, no. 638; Rauoul-Rochette, *Monuments inédits d'antiquité figurée, grecque, étrusque et romaine*, Paris,

1837, Pl. XX, Fig. 2. Cista cover. Three Nereids riding sea-monsters and carrying armor. One rides a hippocamp with finlike feet. Cf. pistrices on Rhodian vase (Fig. 70).

2. *Mon. dell'Inst.*, VIII, 31. Cista cover. Four Nereids with armor riding sea-monsters two of which are hippocamps.
3. *Brit. Mus. Cat. Bronzes*, no. 639. Nereids on sea-monsters, two riding hippocamps (Fig. 84).
4. *Ibid.*, no. 640. Nereids on sea-monsters, one riding a hippocamp.
5. *Ibid.*, no. 648. Cista foot. Above lion's claw foot an imitation Ionic column on which rests a Nereid carrying a helmet and riding a hippocamp.
6. *Mon. dell'Inst.*, IX, Pls. 22-23. Cista cover. Man and woman each on sea-monster.
7. *Ibid.*, Suppl., Pls. 19-20. Cista cover. Two hippocamps with two-tailed merman. Chap. VIII, n. 4.
8. *Ibid.*, Suppl., Pls. 17-18. Cista cover. Hippocamp with sea-monster and merman. Chap. VIII, n. 4.
9. *Ibid.*, VI, Pl. 40. Cista body. Perseus rescuing Andromeda. Above the main picture, a frieze of sea-monsters among which are three hippocamps with flying manes.
10. *Museo Borbonico*, XIV, Pl. 40. Cista cover. Hippocamp with spikes on nose.
11. Gerhard, *Etruskische Spiegel*, I, Berlin, 1848, Pl. V, 3. Cista cover. Hippocamp very badly preserved.
12. *Ibid.*, I, Pl. VII, 3. Cista cover. Hippocamp and *ketos* facing.
13. *Ibid.*, I, Pl. VIII, 3. Cista cover. Two hippocamps facing.
14. *Mon. dell'Inst.*, X, Pl. 29. Cista cover. Hippocamp with *ketos*.
15. Schumacher, *op. cit.*, no. 256. Cista cover. Hippocamp with *ketos*.

E. ETRUSCAN MIRRORS

1. *Brit. Mus. Cat. Bronzes*, no. 624; *Mon. dell'Inst.*, XI, Pl. 8, Fig. 2; Gerhard, *op. cit.*, V, Pl. 112, Fig. 2. Etruscan mirror of the finest period. Nereid riding hippocamp and carrying armor.
2. *Brit. Mus. Cat. Bronzes*, no. 728. Late Etruscan mirror case. Nereid riding hippocamp with pectoral fins in place of legs.
3. Gerhard, *op. cit.*, IV, Pl. 283. Etruscan mirror. Nereid riding hippocamp with elaborate bridle and bit.
4. *Ibid.*, I, Pl. 118. Etruscan mirror. Winged deity, probably Eros, riding hippocamp with pectoral fins in place of legs.
5. *Ibid.*, I, Pl. 119. Etruscan mirror. Design the same as no. 4.

6. *Ibid.*, I, Pl. 103. Etruscan mirror. In exergue, hippocamp and *ketos* facing.
7. *Ibid.*, II, Pl. 215. Etruscan mirror. In exergue, two hippocamps facing.
8. *Ibid.*, II, Pl. 236. Etruscan mirror. In exergue, two hippocamps facing (very careless work).

F. HELLENISTIC RELIEF VASES

1. *Merman* no. 1.
2. *Merman* no. 2.
3. Courby, *op. cit.*, p. 381, Fig. 79, 34. Bowl from Delos. Nereid carrying armor and riding hippocamp.
4. *Ibid.*, p. 405, Fig. 87, 4. Fragment of relief vase from Pergamum. Hippocamp and dolphin.
5. *Brit. Mus. Cat. Vases*, IV, G 43. Askos from Rhodes. Black ware with relief. Bearded figure riding hippocamp with scaly body.
6. Pagenstecher, *op. cit.*, nos. 206 a, b; 207 a, b, c; Calenian gutti. Nereid riding hippocamp and carrying armor.
7. *Ibid.*, no. 37, Pl. VIII; no. 208 a, b; 209 a, b, c, d, e. Calenian vases. Hippocamp and Nereid.
8. *Ibid.*, no. 40. Calenian phiale. Hippocamp.

G. HELLENISTIC COINS

1. Kyzikos. Overbeck, *Griechische Kunstmythologie*, Leipzig, Berlin, 1871-1889, II, Coin Plate 6, 22. Bearded deity riding hippocamp.
2. Locris. *Brit. Mus. Cat. Coins, Central Greece*, p. 6, no. 42. Hippocamp used as decoration on the shield of the lesser Ajax. 338-300 B.C.
3. Coin issued by Pyrrhus of Epeiros. *Brit. Mus. Cat. Coins, Thessaly to Aetolia*, p. 111, no. 8, Pl. XX, 11; I.-B. and K., Pl. XI, Fig. 36; Head, *op. cit.*, Fig. 183. Thetis riding hippocamp and carrying shield. 295-272 B.C. (Figs. 37c & 94).
4. Bruttium. I.-B. and K., Pl. VII, Fig. 25. Type similar to above. Eros on hippocamp's tail shooting arrow at goddess. 280-146 B.C.
5. Cumae. Müller-Wiesler, *Denkmäler der alten Kunst*, Göttingen, 1854-1877, II, 7, 85. Girl in chariot drawn by hippocamps.
6. Syracuse. *Brit. Mus. Cat. Coins, Sicily*, p. 208, no. 514. Head of Persephone with hippocamp behind as symbol. 275-216 B.C.
7. Solus. *Ibid.*, p. 143, no. 1; Hill, *Coins of Ancient Sicily*, London,

1903, p. 141, Fig. 40. Hippocamp with sickle wing and tail pointing downward. Archaic appearance. 275-212 B.C.

8. Coin of Crepeia Family. I.-B. and K., Pl. II, Fig. 37. Poseidon driving a span of hippocamps (Fig. 37d). *ca.* 50 B.C.

H. HELLENISTIC GEMS

1. I.-B. and K., Pl. XXVI, Figs. 4, 5, 6. Hippocamp.
2. *Ibid.*, Pl. XXVI, Fig. 9; *Brit. Mus. Cat. Gems*, no. 1298, Pl. XVIII. Nereid riding hippocamp and holding cuirass.
3. *Brit. Mus. Cat. Finger-Rings*, no. 1261, Pl. XXXI. Bronze ring. Nereid riding hippocamp and carrying armor.
4. Furtwängler, *A.G.*, Pl. XXIX, 23. Eros standing on back of hippocamp with tail ending in dragon's head.
5. *Ibid.*, Pl. XXXIX, 24. Aphrodite, clad in a thin chiton, resting her hand on the back of a hippocamp. Furtwängler believes that this was copied after the Aphrodite of Alkamenes.

III. *THE KETOS*

A. SOUTH ITALIAN VASES

1. Langlotz, *op. cit.*, no. 821, Pl. 238. South Italian pyxis of early style (Fig. 78b). *Ketos* with snaky body (cf. Fig. 78a).
2. *Hippocamp* no. 1. Nereid riding *ketos* with speckled head and neck and long snout.
3. *Hippocamp* no. 3. Nereid riding *ketos* with snaky body.
4. *Hippocamp* no. 4. Two Nereids riding *kete.*
5. Rauoul-Rochette, *op. cit.*, Pl. VI; Inghirami, *op. cit.*, II, Pl. 168. Nereid riding *ketos* and carrying spear.
6. *Hippocamp* no. 7. Nereid on *ketos.*
7. *Hippocamp* no. 8. Nereid on *ketos.*
8. *Hippocamp* no. 6. Nude youth in Phrygian dress riding *ketos*. Below, sea-monster with double dog's head and double tail fin.
9. See Chap. VII, n. 8. Perseus slaying *ketos* with long neck and large ears (Fig. 80).
10. See Chap. VII, n. 10. In foreground, *ketos* with long, horny nose (Fig. 79).
11. See Chap. VII, n. 9. *Ketos* of stout build with head like a modern police dog.

12. *Annali*, 1878, Pl. S. Etruscan cup. Perseus slaying the sea-monster. Only the head of the *ketos* is shown with open denticulated jaw and beard.
13. Ducati, *Arte Etrusca*, Rome and Milan, 1927, p. 97, Fig. 90. Etruscan amphora in Orvieto. On neck, two *kete* facing.
14. See Chap. VII, n. 15. Etruscan sherd. Nereid on *ketos*.
15. Berlin, no. 3442. Apulian amphora. Uncertain sea-monster, either sea-goat or *ketos*.

B. CISTAE FROM PRAENESTE

1. *Hippocamp* no. 1. Nereid riding *ketos* with crest and beard.
2. *Hippocamp* no. 2. Nereid riding *ketos* with beard and forelegs of horse.
3. *Mon. dell'Inst.*, VI-VII, Pl. 63. Cista cover. Nereid riding *ketos*.
4. *Hippocamp* no. 3. Two Nereids riding *kete* with crests and beards (Fig. 84).
5. *Hippocamp* no. 4. Nereid riding *ketos* with wings but no legs.
6. *Hippocamp* no. 6. Bearded man clinging to bridle of *ketos* with beard and horned nose.
7. *Hippocamp* no. 8. *Ketos* with hippocamp and merman.
8. *Hippocamp* no. 9. In frieze, two *kete*. In main picture, only head of *ketos* represented snapping at Perseus.
9. *Mon. dell'Inst.*, VIII, Pls. LVIII-LIX. Cover of gold cista. Four *kete*.
10. *Hippocamp* no. 10. *Museo Borbonico*, XIV, Pl. 40. Cista cover. *Ketos* with long protruding tongue.
11. *Hippocamp* no. 12. Hippocamp and *ketos* facing.
12. *Hippocamp* no. 14. Bearded *ketos* with hippocamp.
13. *Hippocamp* no. 15. *Ketos* with hippocamp.

C. ETRUSCAN MIRRORS

1. Gerhard, *op. cit.*, I, Pl. LXV. Nereid riding *ketos*.
2. *Ibid.*, IV, Pl. 430, 3. *Ketos* with crest and beard.
3. *Ibid.*, IV, Pl. 430, 4. *Ketos* similar to no. 2.
4. *Ibid.*, I, Pl. 64. *Ketos* with crest and beard in scene with Poseidon and Amymone.
5. *Ibid.*, V, Pl. 65. Telamon and Hesione. Head of *ketos* represented with horned nose, beard and crest.
6. *Ibid.*, I, Pl. 85. *Ketos* in exergue.

IV. *SKYLLA*

A. SOUTH ITALIAN VASES

(Cf. Waser, op. cit., pp. 130 ff.)

1. *Ketos* no. 1; Chap. VII, n. 16. Skylla fighting with a hippocamp and slinging stone (Fig. 78a). She wears a chlamys partly wound around her left arm. At her waist, the foreparts of two dogs.
2. Langlotz, *op. cit.*, no. 828 and Pl. 239. South Italian pelike. Skylla with one protome aiming a spear at some imaginary adversary. The body, mostly destroyed, seems to have been scaled.
3. *Ketos* no. 11; Chap. VII, n. 9. Skylla with a trident. There are two protomai at her waist, one stretching upward and the other lowered.
4. *Brit. Mus. Cat. Vases*, IV, F 218; Lenormant-deWitte, *op. cit.*, III, Pl. 36; *C.V.A.*, Brit. Mus. VII, Group IV Ea, Pl. 8, 11. Campanian hydria. Skylla brandishing a steering oar and an octopus. She has a feathery girdle beneath which is a single protome of dragonlike aspect. Her huge tail is twisted and coiled.
5. See Chap. VII, n. 8 (*Santangelo*, no. 708; *Mon. dell'Inst.*, IX, 38). Skylla surrounded by the protomai of six dogs attached to a sort of apron (Fig. 80).
6. *Hippocamp* no. 3. Skylla with two protomai carrying a Nereid on her back. Like Hellenistic representations of Skylla, a dragon's head takes the place of the tail.
7. See Chap. VII, n. 13. Bacchic vase in Palermo. At right of principal group, Skylla with one protome and with an oar over her shoulder.

B. HELLENISTIC TERRACOTTAS AND PLASTIC VASES

(Cf. Waser, op. cit., pp. 133 ff.)

1. *Brit. Mus. Cat. Terracottas*, D 92. Terracotta statuette from Canosa. Upper body of Skylla, nude, with drapery over one arm.
2. *Ibid.*, D 187. Prochoos. On front plastic figure of Skylla. Her body terminates on either side in the coiled body of a serpent, one ending in a serpent's head, the other in a serpent's tail.
3. *Collection J. Gréau, Catalogue des terres cuites grecques, vases peints et marbres antiques* (Froehner), Paris, 1891, no. 87, Pl. 2; *Arch. Anz.*, 1892, p. 103. Vase from Canosa. On front, plastic figure of Skylla, winged, with three protomai and two fish-tails. Her arm is raised in a gesture of pleading.

4. Metropolitan Museum. 11. 43. Similar vase with plastic figure of Skylla.
5. *Brit. Mus. Cat. Terracottas,* D 204; *Mon. dell'Inst.,* III, 52, 1. Two-handled Apulian flask. On each side, medallion of Skylla in low relief. The body terminates in two twisting fish-tails which each end in the head of a marine monster. In her right hand a sword, in her left a scabbard. *ca.* 300 B.C.
6. *Berlin,* no. 3592. Circular flask from Apulia. On front, design similar to above.
7. Levi, *Le Terracotte figurate del Museo Nazionale di Napoli,* Florence, 1926, p. 68, no. 287 (Inv. 16270, 16271, 16273), Fig. 63. Circular flasks from Canosa. On both sides designs similar to above.
8. *Mon. dell'Inst.,* III, 52, 8. Circular flask. Skylla with two fish-tails ending in dogs' heads. In each hand a torch.
9. *Brit. Mus. Cat. Terracottas,* D 206. Cover of large Apulian pyxis. Medallion of Skylla in low relief. Design similar to nos. 4, 5, 6 and 7 above. *ca.* 300 B.C.
10. *Mon. dell'Inst.,* III, 52, 2. Pagenstecher, *op. cit.,* no. 18a, Fig. 12. Calenian phiale. Skylla in low relief with two protomai under her girdle and two coiled fish-tails. She is slinging a stone and a snake is wound around her body. Also Pagenstecher, *op. cit.,* no. 18b.
11. Pagenstecher, *op. cit.,* no. 196a, b, c. Calenian gutti. Skylla.
12. *Ibid.,* no. 126a, b, Fig. 36. Calenian omphalos cups. Odysseus' adventure with the Sirens and Skylla. A two-tailed Skylla with an oar over her shoulder is seizing a man who clings to the ship. There is an uncatalogued example of this design in the British Museum.
13. Courby, *op. cit.,* Fig. 70, 23; Watzinger, *Ath. Mitt.,* 1901, p. 65, no. 2. Hellenistic sherd with design in relief. Skylla and the companions of Odysseus (one man with head missing is preserved). Skylla has three protomai and two fish-tails ending in dragons' heads.
14. *Brit. Mus. Cat. Vases,* IV, G 99. Megarian bowl. Between groups of combatants, Skylla with serpent and forepart of dog springing from her body.
15. *Brit. Mus. Cat. Vases,* IV, G 179. Red ware vase with reliefs. This vase has twisted handles ending in female heads on each side of which is a snake's head. These may be representations of Skylla. Cf. also p. 87 for Apulian askoi with plastic figures of Skylla (Fig. 83).

PLATES

PLATE I

FIG. 1. Akkadian Seal Cylinder. The boat of the sun-god.

FIG. 2. Seal Cylinder of the time of Gudea. Man-fish and goat-fish.

FIG. 3. Relief from Tell Halaf. Man-fish.

FIG. 4. Relief from the Palace of Sargon. Man-fish.

FIG. 5. Paris. Louvre. Copper Plaque. Deity in fish-skin cloak.

FIG. 6. Berlin. Deity in fish-skin cloak.

FIG. 7. Paris. Louvre. Kassite Boundary Stone. Goat-fish.

FIG. 8. Imhoof Collection. Roman Coins. Capricorn.

PLATE II

FIG. 9. Candia. Painted Pinax. Hero wrestling with sea-monster.

FIG. 10. Athens. National Museum. Bronze Plaque from Olympia. Herakles wrestling with the Old Man of the Sea.

FIG. 11. Oxford. Ashmolean Museum. Bronze Matrix from Corfu. Merman swimming.

FIG. 12. Paris. Louvre. Painted Terracotta Statuette from Tanagra. Two mermen in antithetical composition.

FIG. 13. Island Gem from Melos. Winged merman.

FIG. 14. London. British Museum. Island Gem. Herakles wrestling with the Old Man of the Sea.

FIG. 15. Cagliari, Sardinia. Graeco-Phoenician Gems from Tharros. Sea-monsters and a dolphin-rider.

FIG. 16. Berlin. Gold Fish from Vettersfelde. Merman with fishes.

PLATE III

FIG. 17 a. London. British Museum. Detail from Corinthian Vase. Merman treading water.

b. Paris. Louvre. Detail from Corinthian Vase. Merman splashing in the surf.

FIG. 18 a. Brussels. Corinthian Vase. Winged monsters which may be a variant of the merman type.

b. Syracuse. Detail from Corinthian Vase. The same.

FIG. 19. Akkadian Seal Cylinder. God of vegetation.

FIG. 20. Cassel. Royal Museum. Klazomenian Vase. Merman.

FIG. 21. Castle Ashby. Northampton Collection. Klazomenian Vase. Merman.

FIG. 22. Paris. Bibliothèque Nationale. Pontic Vase. Merman.

FIG. 23. Rome. Conservatori Palace. Pontic Vase. Men with dolphins' tails.

PLATE IV

FIG. 24. Paris. Louvre. Detail from black-figured Lekythos. Probably Boeotian. Herakles and Halios Geron.

FIG. 25. Athens. National Museum. Early Attic Vase. Herakles and Halios Geron.

FIG. 26. Rhodes. Detail of "Little Master" Cup from cremation tomb, Ialysos. Merman swimming.

FIG. 27. New York. Metropolitan Museum. Attic black-figured Vase. Herakles and Triton.

FIG. 28. Athens. Acropolis Museum. Poros Pediment.

FIG. 29. Rhodes. Ivory Plaque from sixth-century tomb, Ialysos. Fish-bodied "siren".

PLATE V

FIG. 30. Copenhagen. Minoan Prism Seal. Pair of hippocamps.

FIG. 31. Athens. National Museum. Gold Ornament from Mycenae. Hippocamp.

FIG. 32. Island Gem from Melos. Hippocamp.

FIG. 33. London. British Museum. Island Gem. Hippocamp.

FIG. 34. Island Gem from Melos. Hippocamp.

FIG. 35. Würzburg. Pontic Vase. Hippocamp.

FIG. 36. London. British Museum. Attic black-figured Cylix. Old man riding hippocamp.

FIG. 37a. Imhoof Collection. Coin of Tarentum. Winged hippocamp.

b. Copenhagen. Silver Coin of Tyre. Deity riding winged hippocamp.

c. Imhoof Collection. Coin of Pyrrhus. Thetis riding hippocamp and carrying the arms of Achilles.

d. Imhoof Collection. Coin of Crepereia Family. Poseidon driving a span of hippocamps.

FIG. 38. Berlin. Corinthian Vase. Perseus rescuing Andromeda from the sea-monster.

FIG. 39. Candia. Clay Seal Impression from Knossos. Boatman having an encounter with a sea-monster.

FIG. 40. Collection of Sir Arthur Evans. Island Gem from Epidaurus Limera. *Ketos* swimming beneath war galley.

PLATE VI

FIG. 41. Berlin. Clay Pinax. Deity riding *ketos*.

FIG. 42. Boston. Museum of Fine Arts. Etruscan Bronze Statuette. Merman.

FIG. 43. New York. Metropolitan Museum. Etruscan Bronze Ornament. Merman with two tails.

FIG. 44. Villa Giulia. Etruscan Terracotta Antefix. Merman with two tails.

FIG. 45. Paris. Louvre. Etruscan Ivory Relief. Merman with hooked nose.

FIG. 46. Munich. Glyptotek. Etruscan Bronze Relief from Perugia. Man with fins on his garment. Hippocamp.

FIG. 47. London. British Museum. Etruscan Bronze Handle. Two mermen.

PLATE VII

FIG. 48a. Corneto. Tomba del Mare. Pediment Painting. Mermen and hippocamp.

FIG. 48b. Corneto. Tomba dei Tori. Pediment Painting. Hippocamp and sea-dog.

FIG. 48c. Corneto. Tomba del Barone and Tomba dei Tori. Pediment Paintings. Hippocamps.

FIG. 49. Paris. Bibliothèque Nationale. Etruscan Bronze Statuette from Perugia. Mermaid.

FIG. 50. Perugia. Bronze Relief from Perugia. Fish-tailed siren.

FIG. 51. Tarquinia. Museo Nationale. Cult Stairway. Winged hippocamps.

FIG. 52. Rome. Villa Giulia. Tufa Statue. Boy riding hippocamp.

PLATE VIII

FIG. 53. Naples. Sculptured Group from Locri. Merman supporting one of the Dioscuri on horseback.

FIG. 54. London. British Museum. Attic red-figured Vase. Herakles wrestling with Acheloos.

FIG. 55. Attic red-figured Vase. Herakles wrestling with Triton. Present whereabouts unknown.

FIG. 56. London. British Museum. Gem of the severe style. Herakles and Triton.

FIG. 57. Paris. Louvre. Melian Relief. Theseus and Triton.

FIG. 58a. London. British Museum. Coins of Itanos. Mermen.

FIG. 58b. London. British Museum. Coins of Itanos. Mermen and *kete*.

PLATE IX

FIG. 59a. London. British Museum. Coin of Kyzikos. Merman with tunny fish.

b. Bologna. Coin of Campanian Cumae. Merman with mussel shell.

c. Gotha. Coin of Itanos, Crete. Merman spearing fish with trident.

d. Coin of Corinth. Head of Athena with merman behind swinging trident.

e. Paris. Unidentified Phoenician Stater, perhaps from Azotos. Merman with trident and wreath.

f. Imhoof Collection. Silver coin of Arados, Phoenicia. Merman with fish in each hand.

g. The same as f.

h. Turin. Bronze Coin of Corinth. Aphrodite riding in a chariot drawn by a span of mermen. Roman period.

i. Imhoof Collection. Bronze Coin of Corinth. Poseidon riding in a chariot drawn by a span of mermen. Roman period.

j. Paris. Bronze Coin of Kyzikos. Ichthyocentaur with oar and fish. Roman period.

k. Vienna and Munich. Bronze Coin of Nikomedeia. Ichthyocentaur with oar and fish.

FIG. 60. Paris. Louvre. Relief Plaque from Melos. Winged hippocamp.

FIG. 61. Paris. Louvre. Cover of Pyxis from Eretria. Nereid on hippocamp.

FIG. 62. Baltimore. Walters Gallery. Painted Marble Vase. Amphitrite and Poseidon in chariot drawn by hippocamps. In front, Triton.

PLATE X

FIG. 63. London. British Museum. Coin of Sybrita. Winged hippocamp.

FIG. 64. Athens. National Museum. Melian Relief. Nereid with armor riding on a *ketos*.

FIG. 65. Mosaic found at Olynthos. Nereids riding *kete* and carrying the armor of Achilles.

FIG. 66. London. British Museum. Melian Relief. Skylla.

FIG. 67. Berlin. Gem. Skylla.

FIG. 68a. Imhoof Collection. Silver Obol from Allifae in Samnium. Skylla with cuttle fish.

b. Collection of Luynes and Arolsen. Coin of Campanian Cumae. Skylla with clawlike hand.

c. Imhoof Collection. Tetradrachm of Syracuse. In exergue, Skylla with trident.

d. Collection of Orlando in Palermo. Tetradrachm of Akragas. Below crab, Skylla beckoning.

e. Imhoof Collection. Denar of Pompey the Great. Skylla fighting with oar.

PLATE XI

FIG. 69. Bologna. Museo Civico. Grave Stele from Felsina. Hippocamp in combat with serpent.

FIG. 70. Munich. Marble Vase found at Rhodes. Frieze of Nereids on sea-animals.

FIG. 71. Ostia. Small Marble Statue of Nereid or Tritoness, after Skopas.

FIG. 72. Dresden. Small Marble Statue of Aphrodite with a supporting Triton, perhaps after Skopas.

FIG. 73. Mosaic Pavement found at Olynthos. Nereids riding sea-animals.

FIG. 74. Birmingham, England. Graeco-Scythian Fibula from the Crimaea. Sheath surmounted by hippocamp.

FIG. 75. Baltimore. Collection of D. M. Robinson. Modern Cast of the Seal of Larissa Kremaste. Thetis riding a hippocamp. Skylla.

PLATE XII

FIG. 76. Boston. Museum of Fine Arts. Gold Ring. Nereid riding a hippocamp.

FIG. 77a. London. British Museum. Silver Coin from unknown Etruscan city. Hippocamp.

b. Copper Coin of Syracuse. Winged hippocamp.

FIG. 78a. Würzburg. South Italian Pyxis. Skylla.

FIG. 78b. The same. *Ketos*.

FIG. 79. Goluchow. Czartoryski Museum. Early South Italian Amphora. Nereid on hippocamp. *Ketos*.

FIG. 80. Naples. South Italian Amphora. Nereid on hippocamp. Skylla. *Ketos*.

FIG. 81. Rome. Villa Giulia. Faliscan Krater. Hippocamp and *ketos*.

PLATE XIII

FIG. 82. Boston. Museum of Fine Arts. Faliscan Stamnos. Handles in the form of hippocamps with tails entwined.

FIG. 83. Boston. Museum of Fine Arts. Apulian Askos. Plastic representation of Skylla.

FIG. 84. London. British Museum. Cover of Cista. Nereids riding sea-monsters.

FIG. 85. Berlin. Staatliche Museen. Small frieze of sea-monsters.

FIG. 86. Berlin. Gem. Two-tailed merman.

FIG. 87. Peiraeus Museum. Grave Stele. Two mermen.

PLATE XIV

FIG. 88a, b. Athens. National Museum. The Veil of Despoina from Lykosura. Nereids riding sea-animals.

FIG. 89a, b, c. Rome. Palazzo Conservatori. Marble Foot. Sandal decorated with frieze of sea-monsters and Nereids.

FIG. 90. Athens. National Museum. Frieze from Lamia. Sea-monsters and Nereids.

FIG. 91. Berlin. Bronze Mirror from Eretria. Skylla seizing the companions of Odysseus.

PLATE XV

FIG. 92. Athens. National Museum. Bronze Relief from Dodona. Skylla.

FIG. 93. Gem. Skylla seizing a comrade of Odysseus.

FIG. 94. Imhoof Collection. Didrachme of Pyrrhos. Thetis riding a hippocamp and carrying the shield of Achilles.

FIG. 95a. Cassel Collection. Gem. Eros riding a hippocamp.

b. London. British Museum. Sard. Nereid riding a hippocamp and carrying a cuirass.

c. London. British Museum. Sard. Poseidon driving a span of hippocamps.

d. Amethyst from Collection of Lorenzo de Medici. Nereid riding a hippocamp. Another hippocamp swimming in front.

FIG. 96. Interior of Tomb of the Reliefs at Cervetri. Skylla (?).

FIG. 97. Etruscan Terracotta Sarcophagus from Tuscany. Skylla throwing a stone.

PLATE XVI

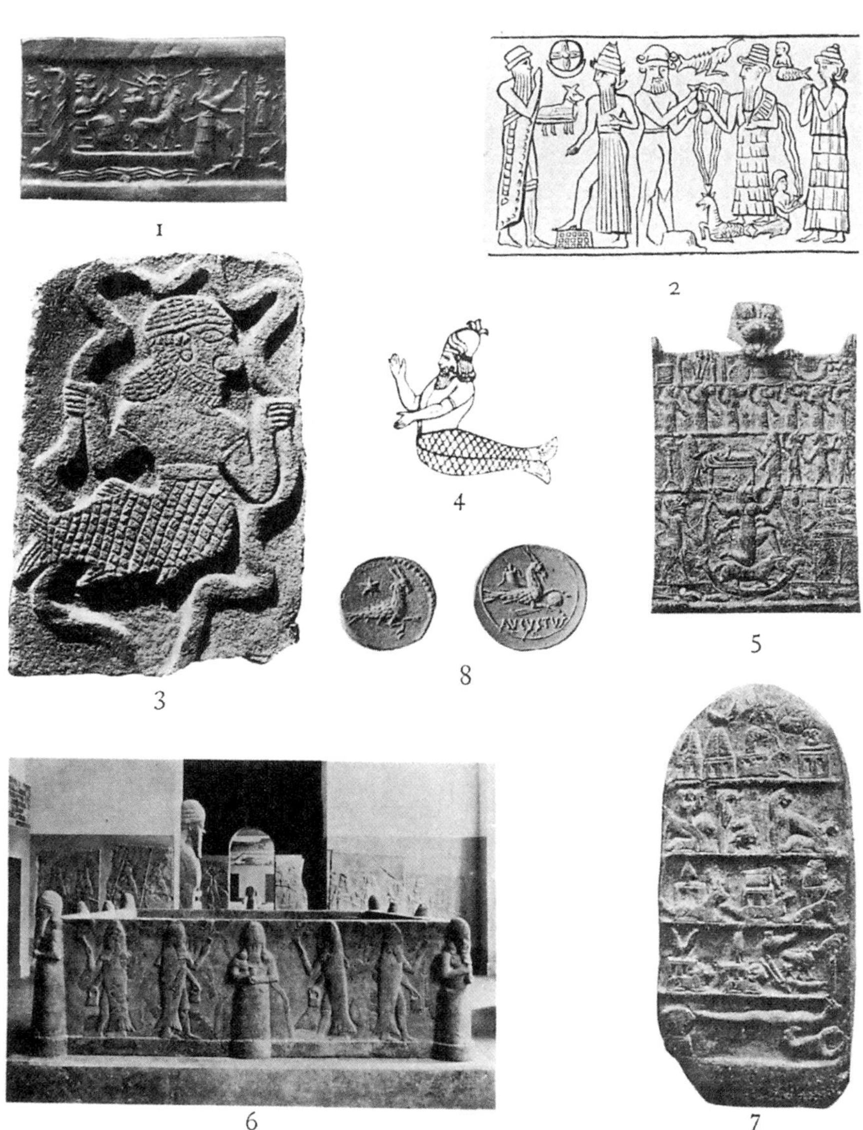

PLATE I

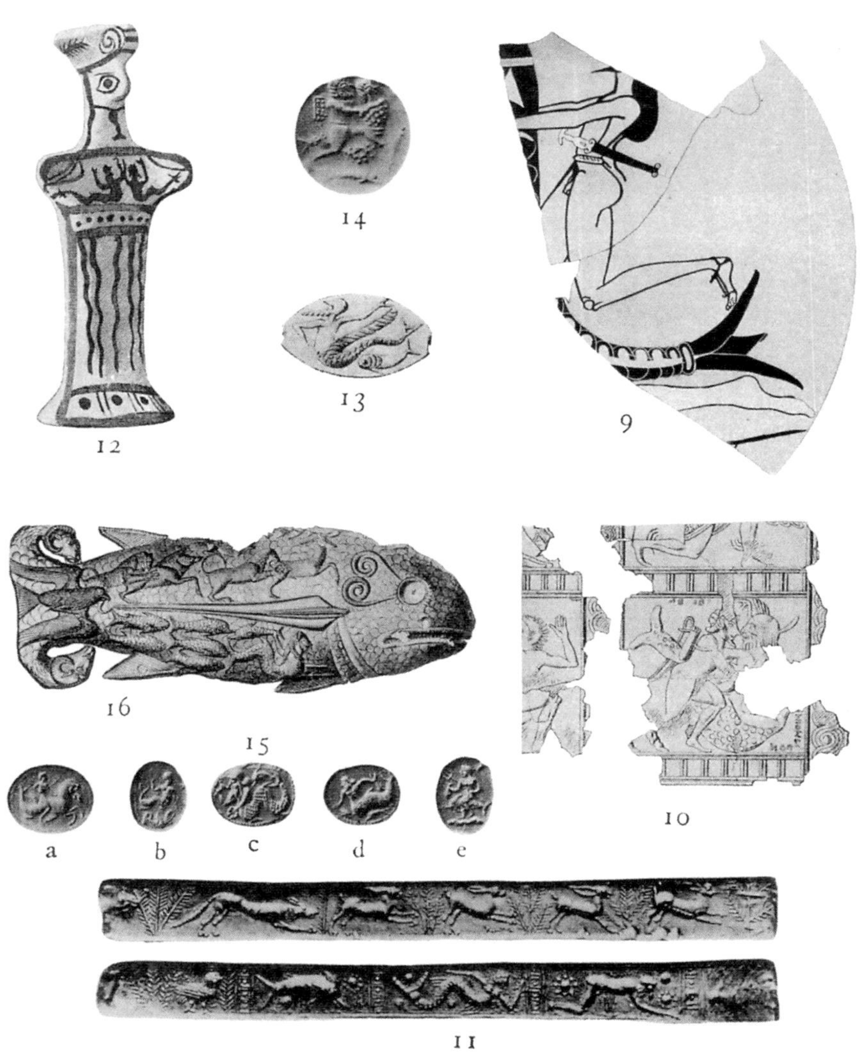

PLATE II

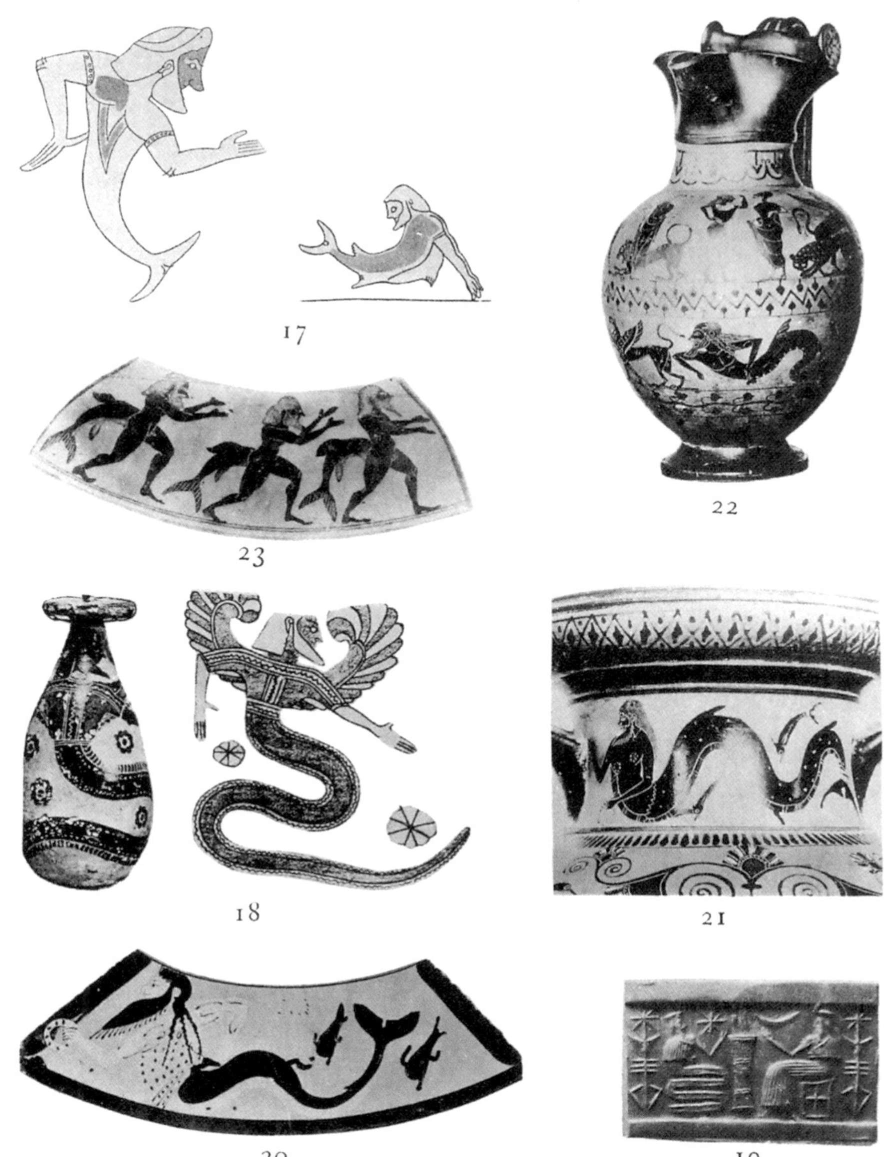
17
22
23
18
21
20
19

PLATE III

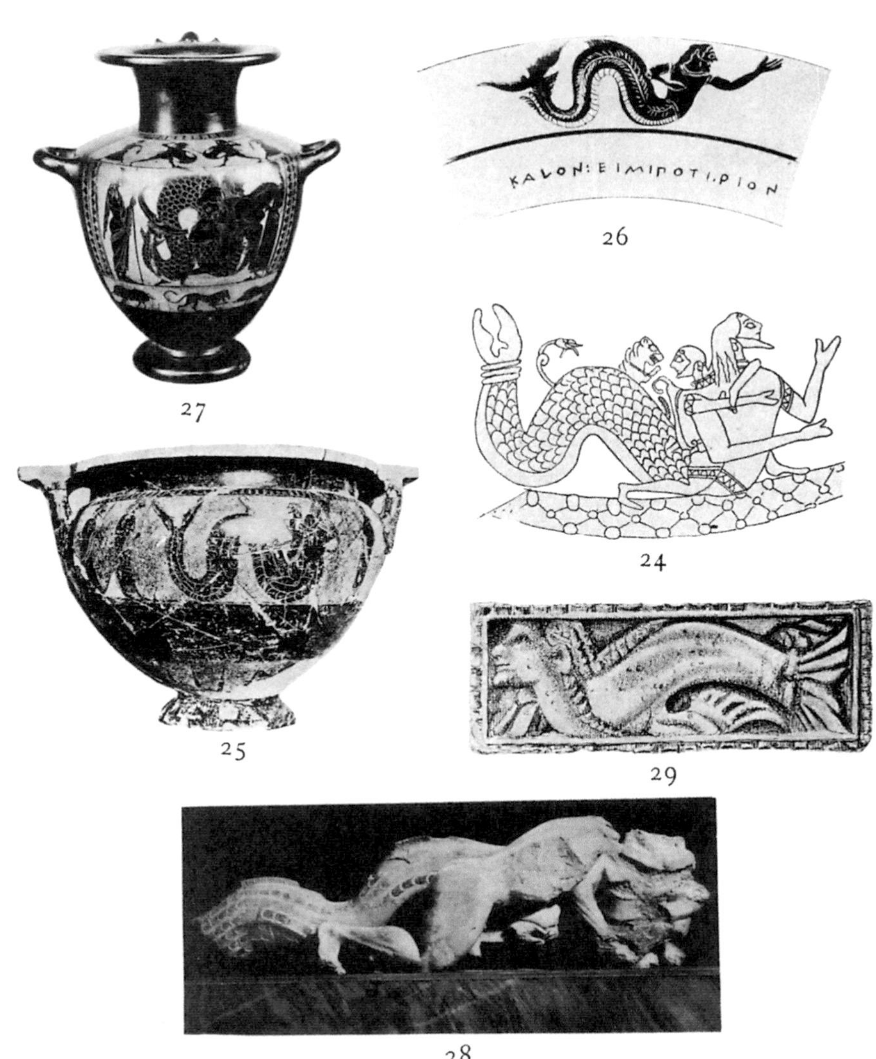

PLATE IV

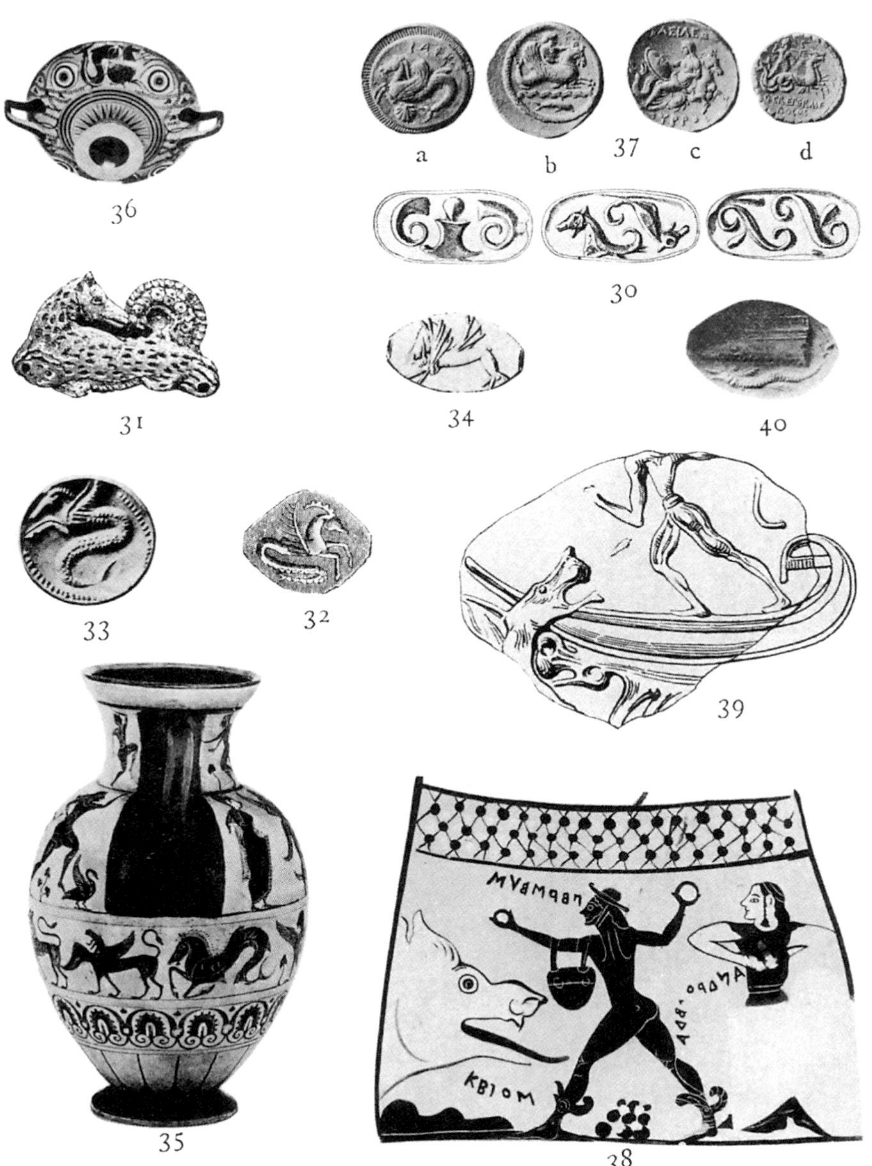

PLATE V

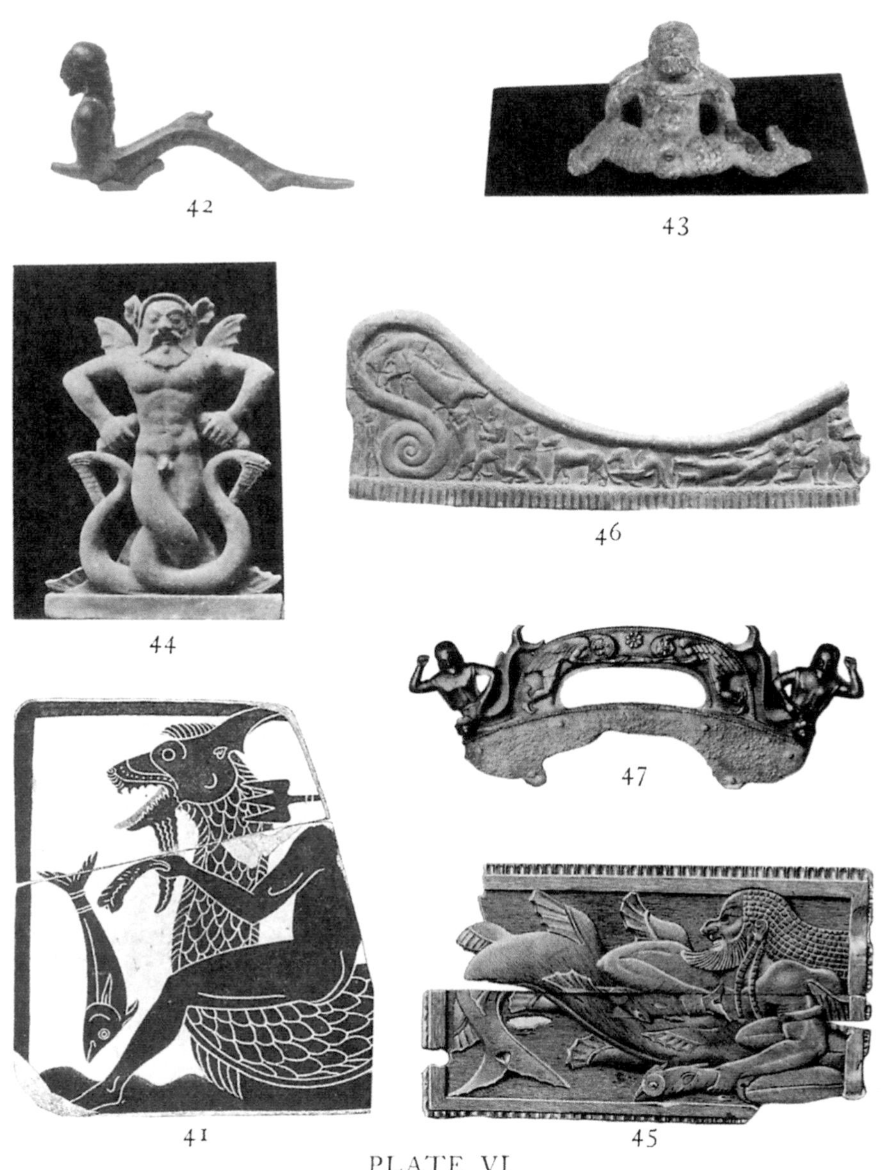

42 43 44 46 47 41 45

PLATE VI

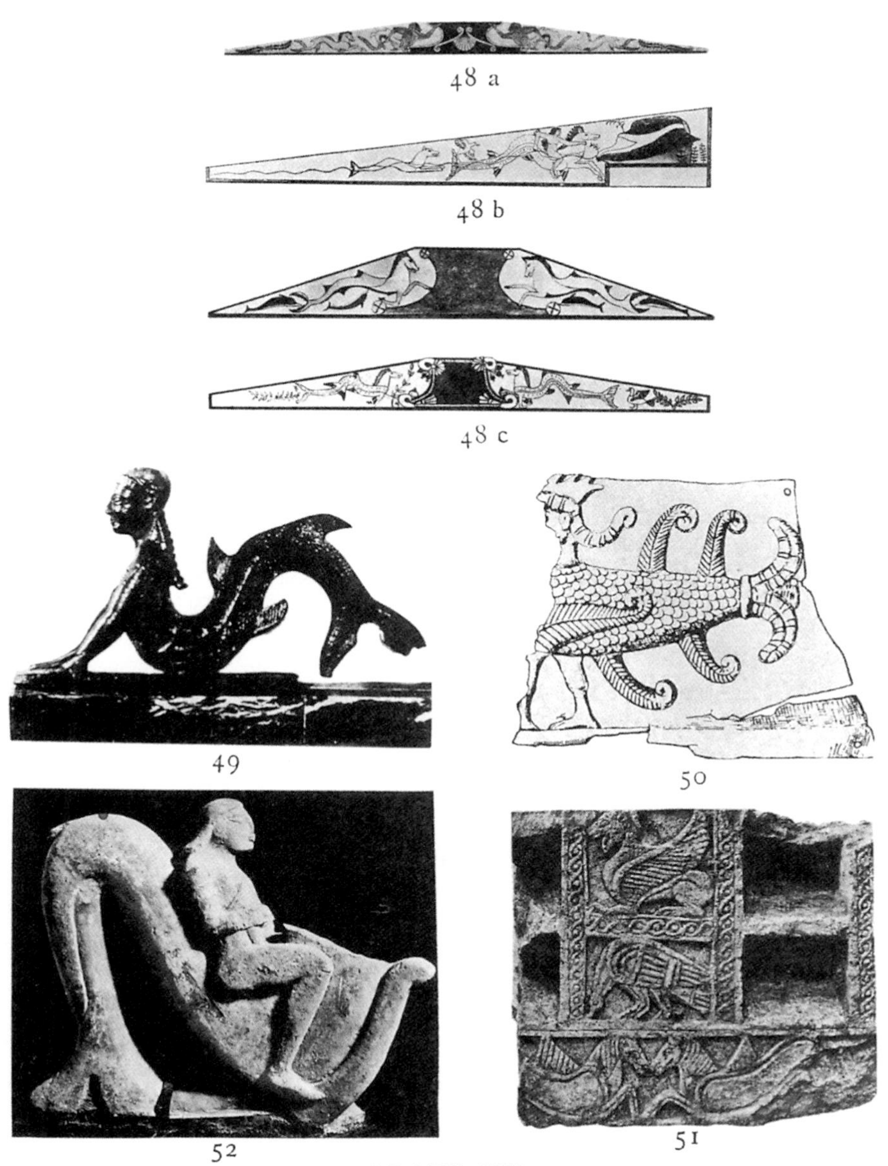

48 a

48 b

48 c

49

50

52

51

PLATE VII

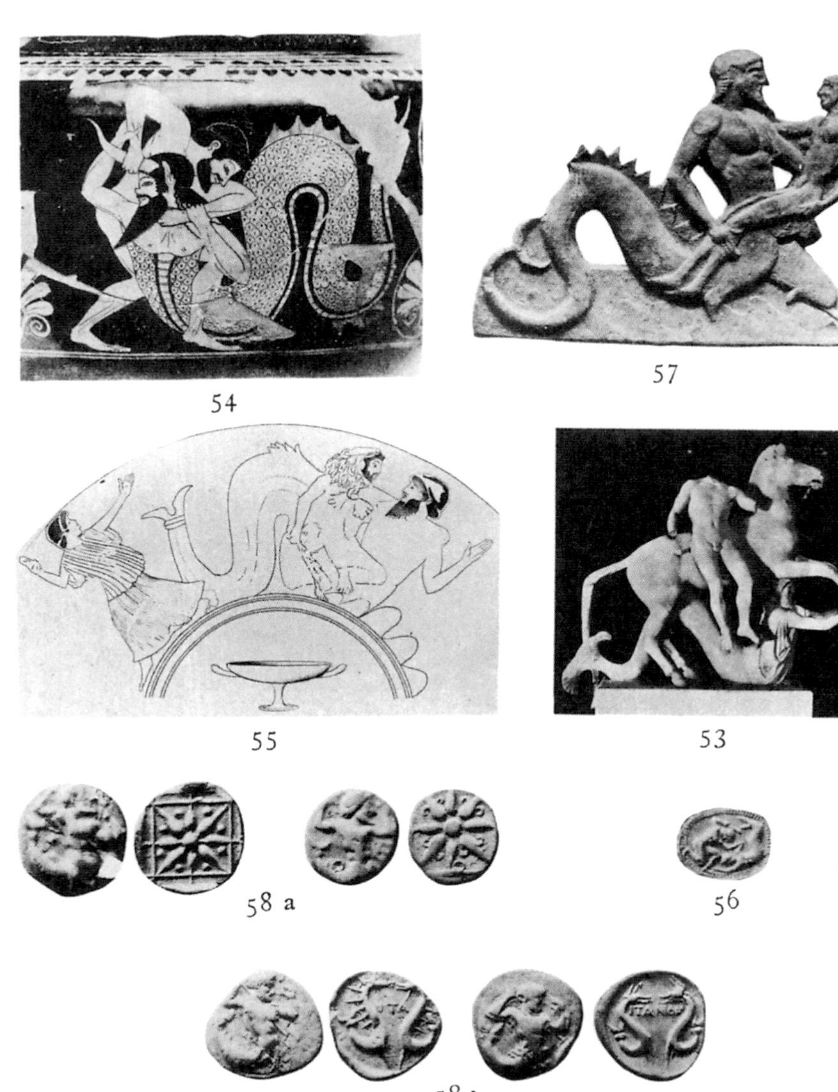
54 57 55 53 58 a 56 58 b

PLATE VIII

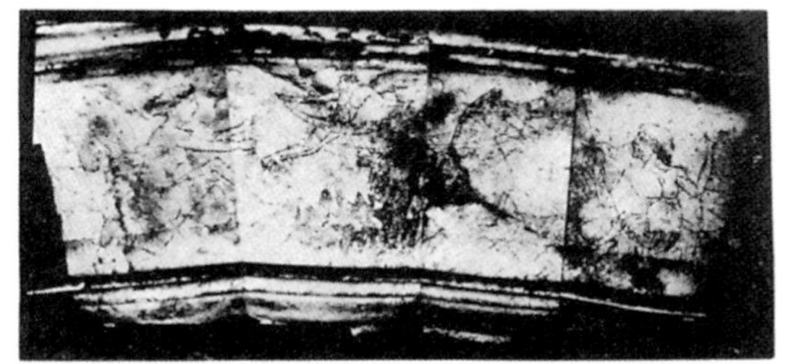

62

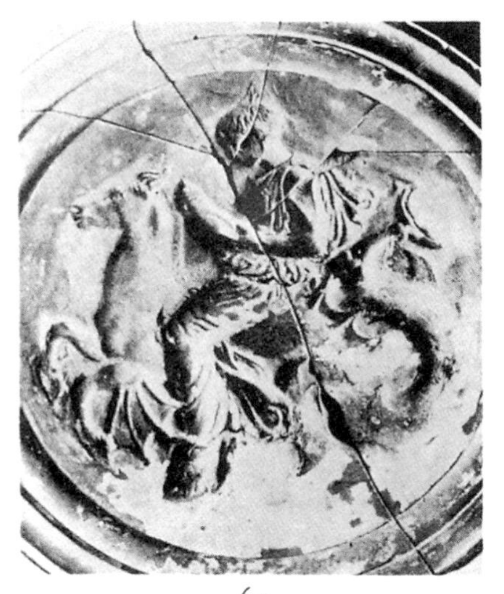

61

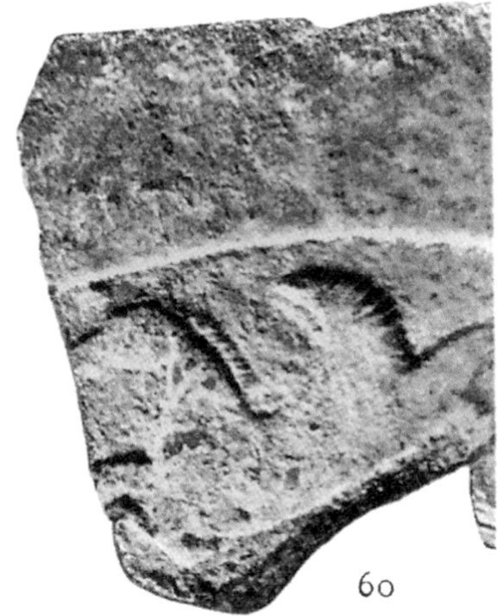

60

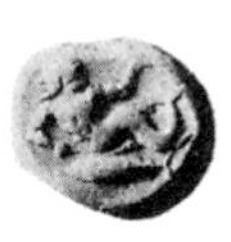
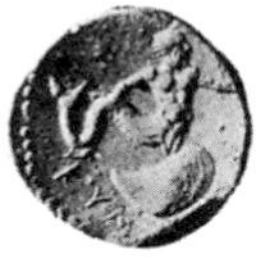
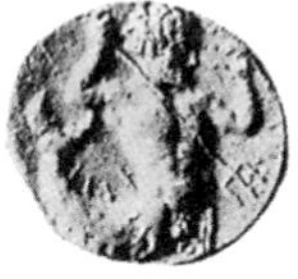
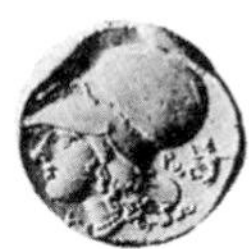
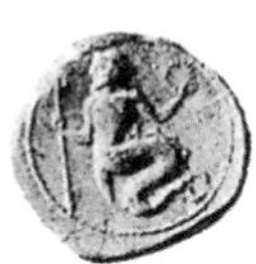
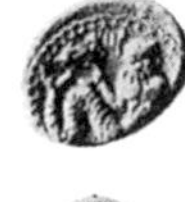
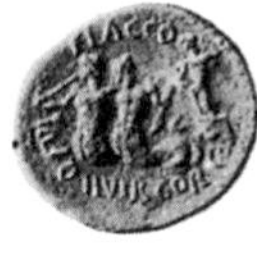
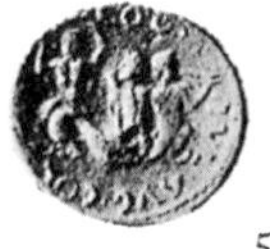
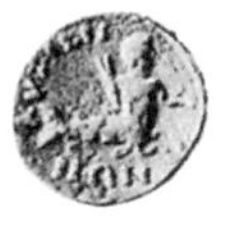
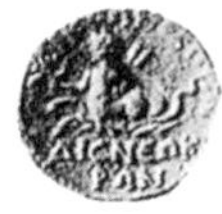

59

PLATE IX

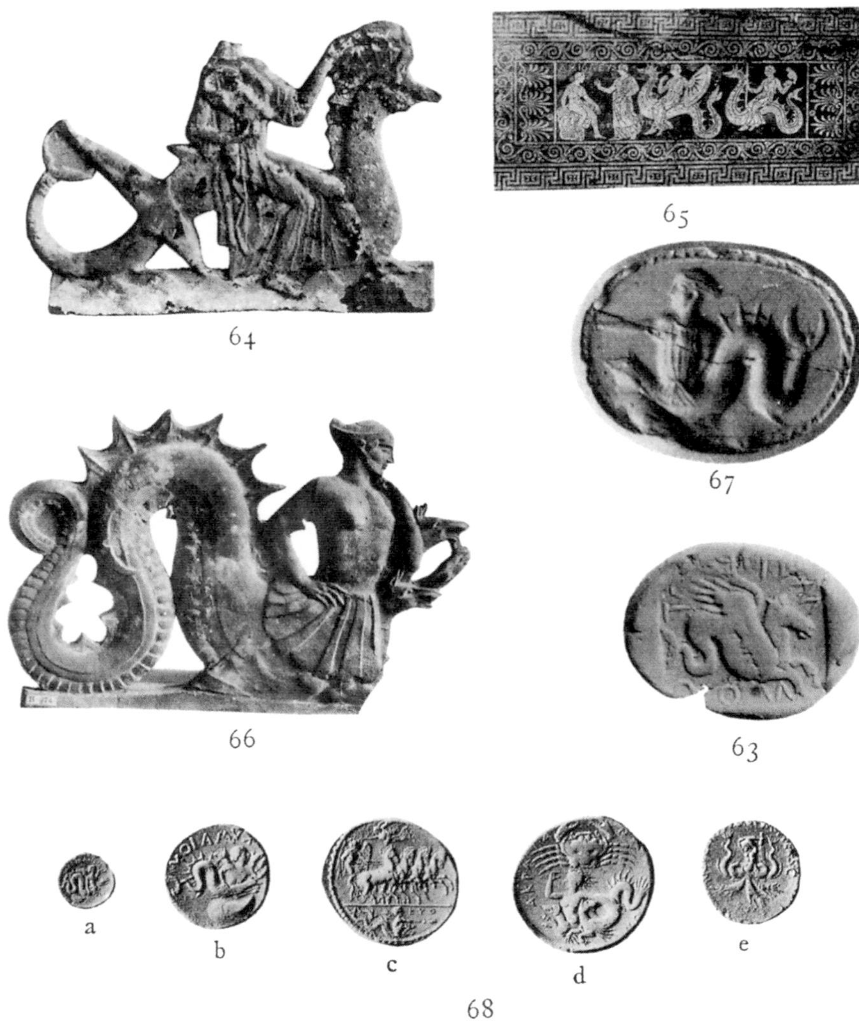

PLATE X

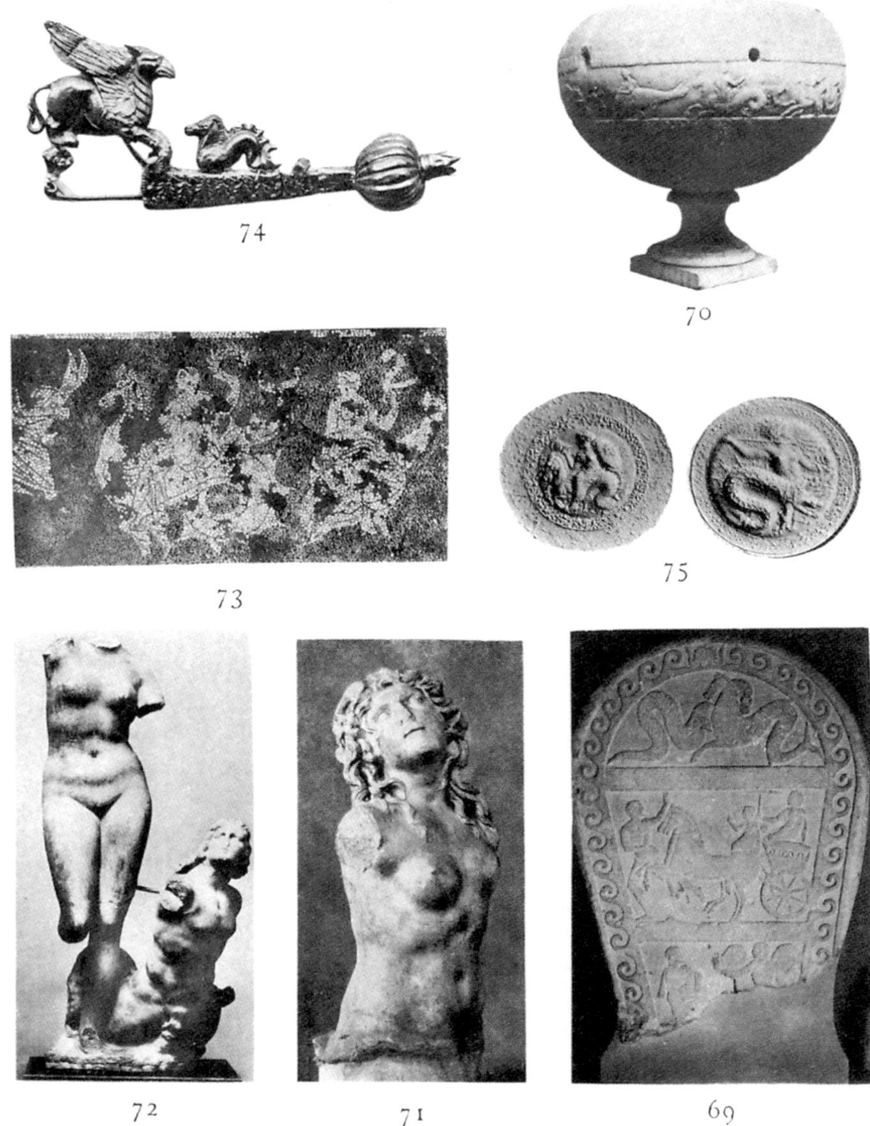

74

70

73

75

72

71

69

PLATE XI

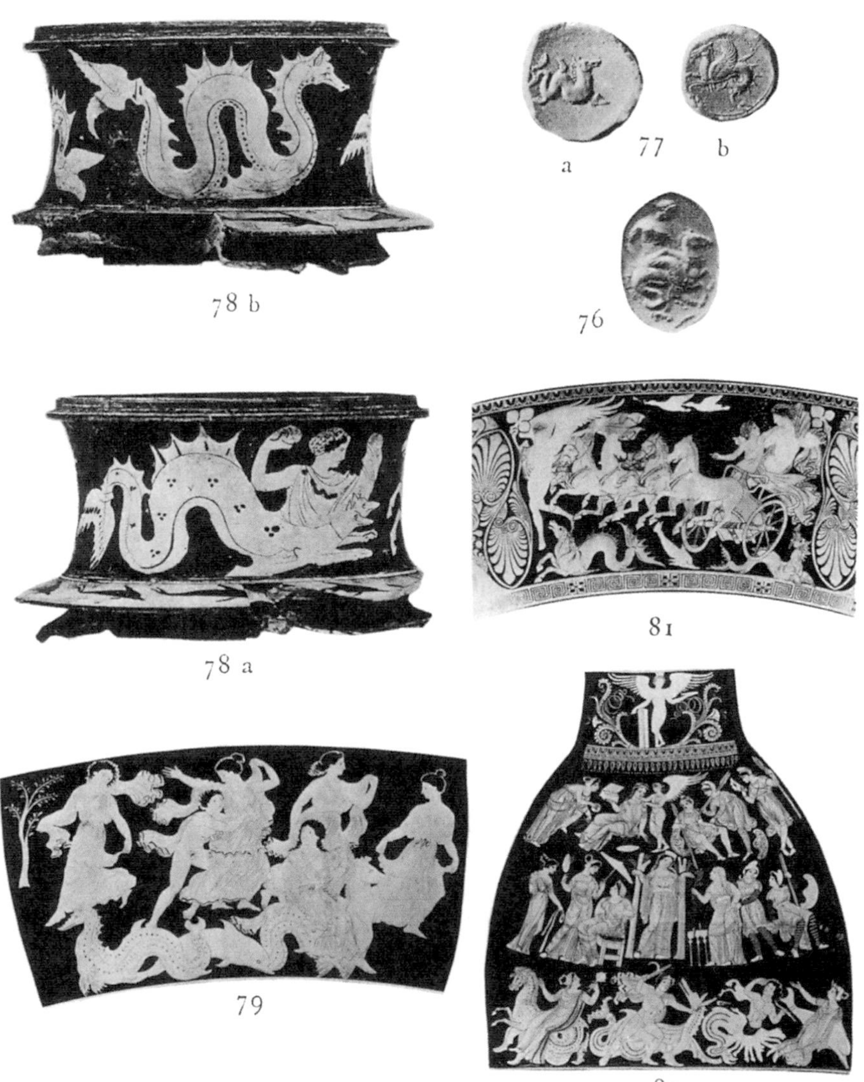

PLATE XII

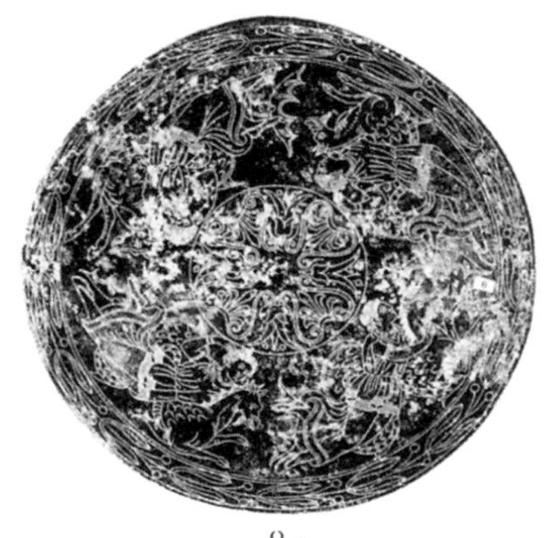

84

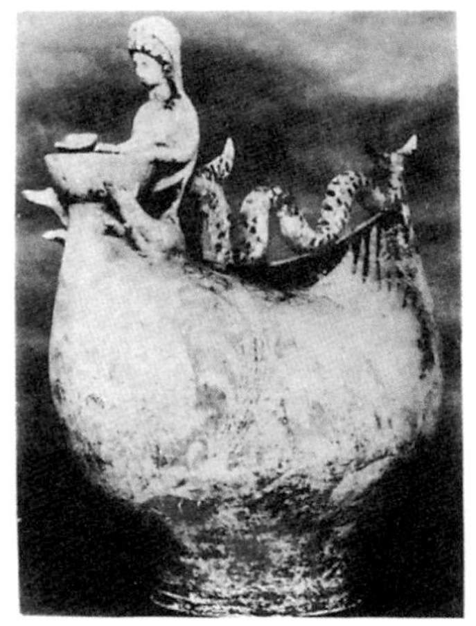

83

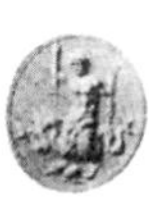

86

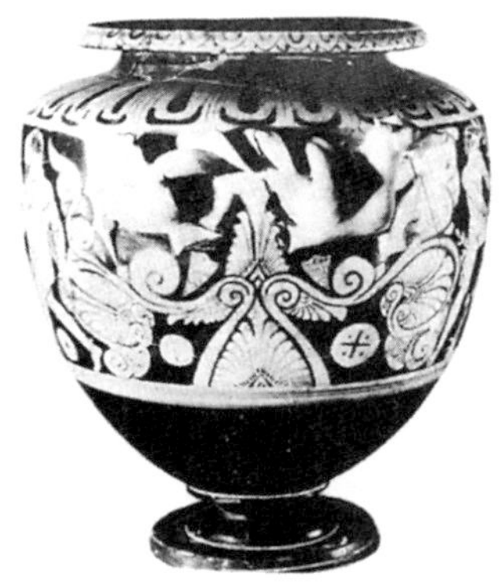

82

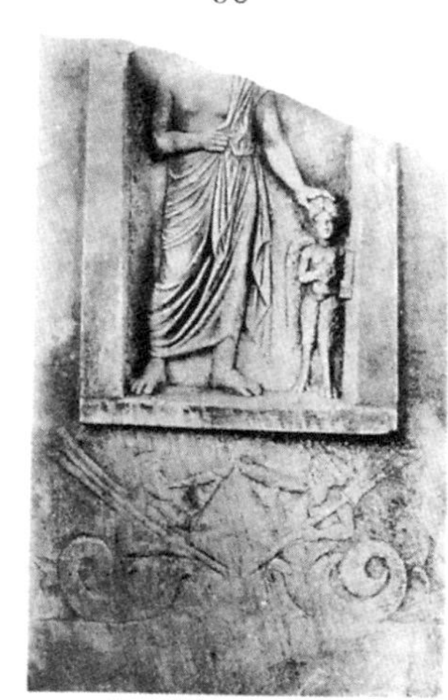

87

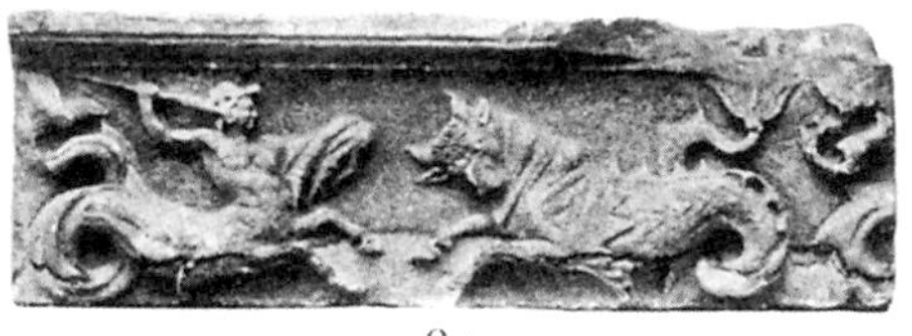

85

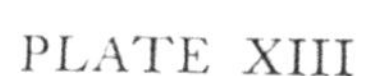

PLATE XIII

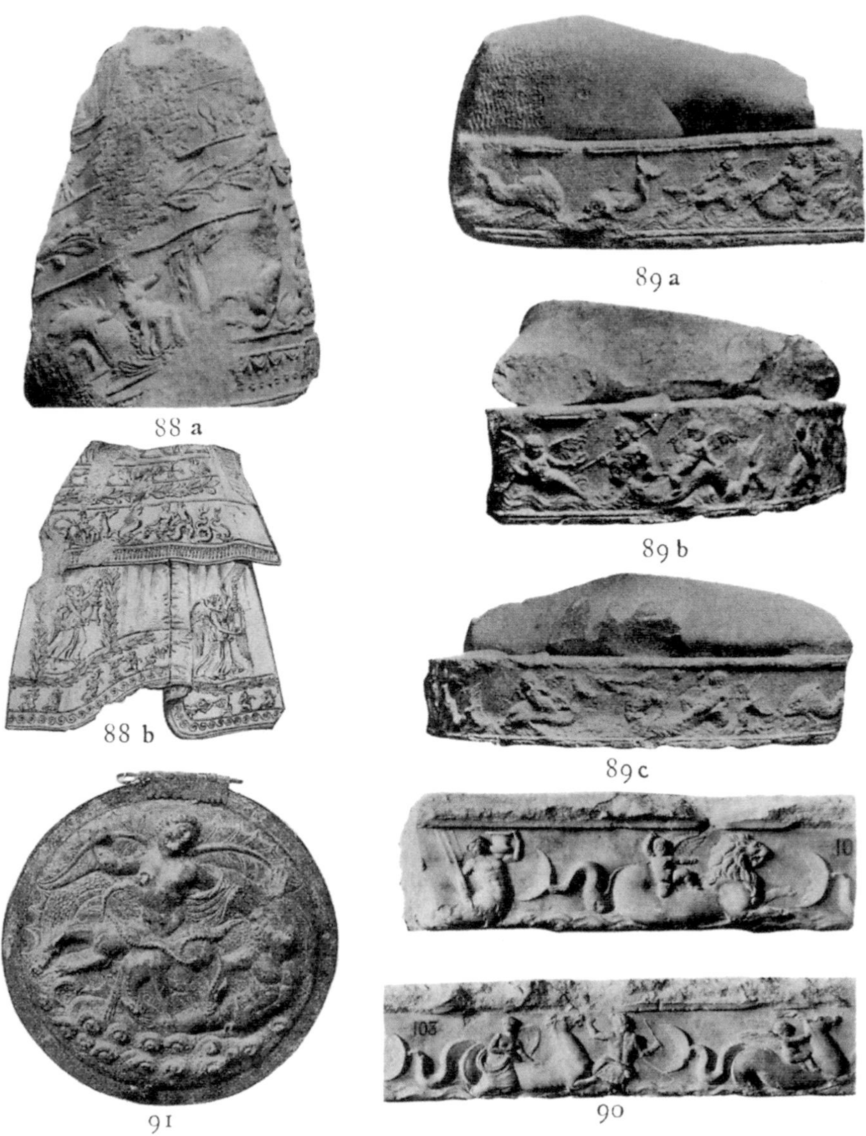

88 a

88 b

89 a

89 b

89 c

91

90

PLATE XIV

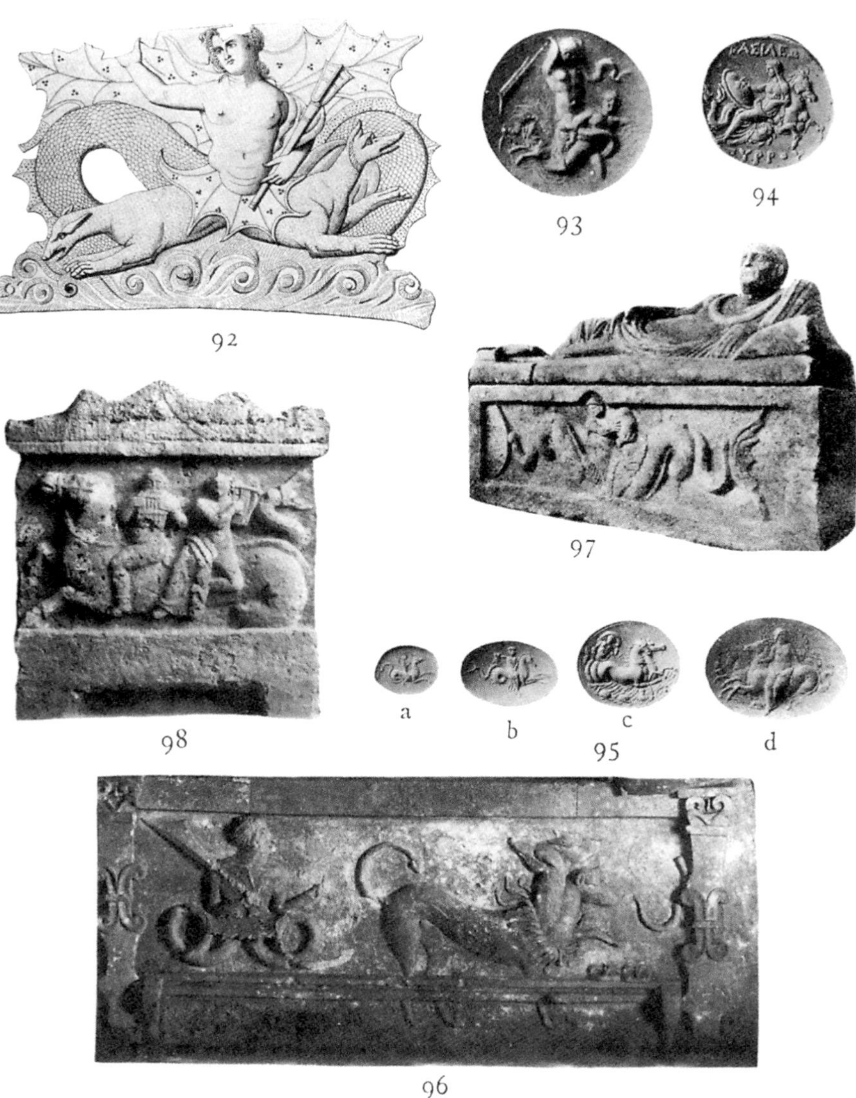

PLATE XV

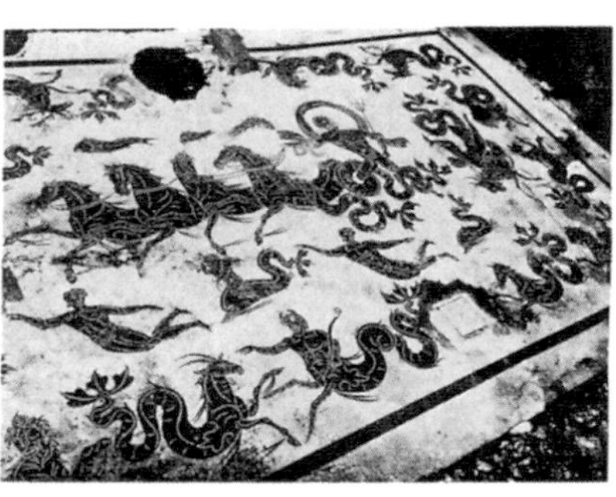

102

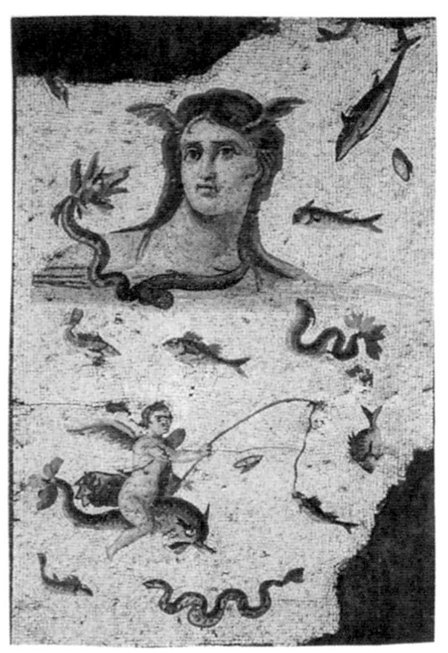

103

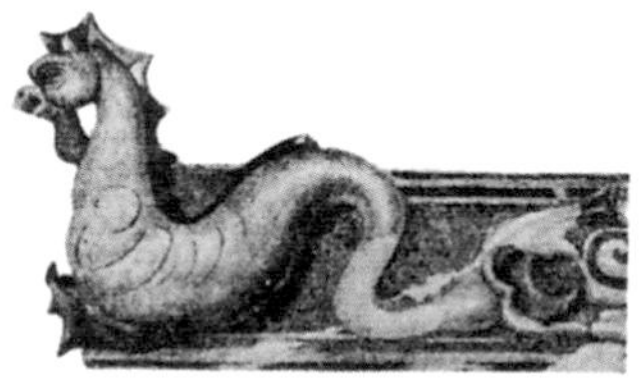

100

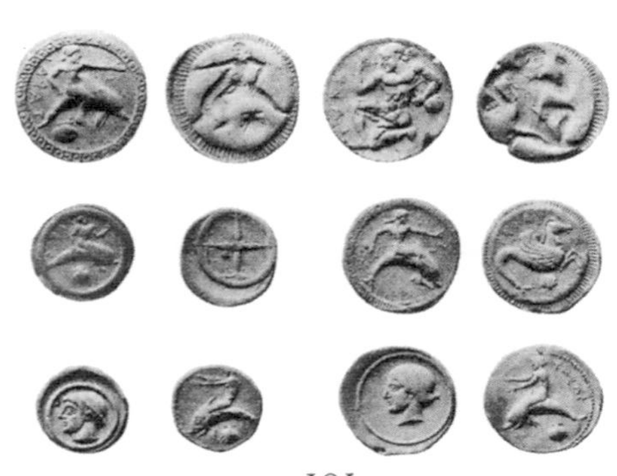

101

99

PLATE XVI

INDEX

INDEX

Coachwhip Publications

CoachwhipBooks.com

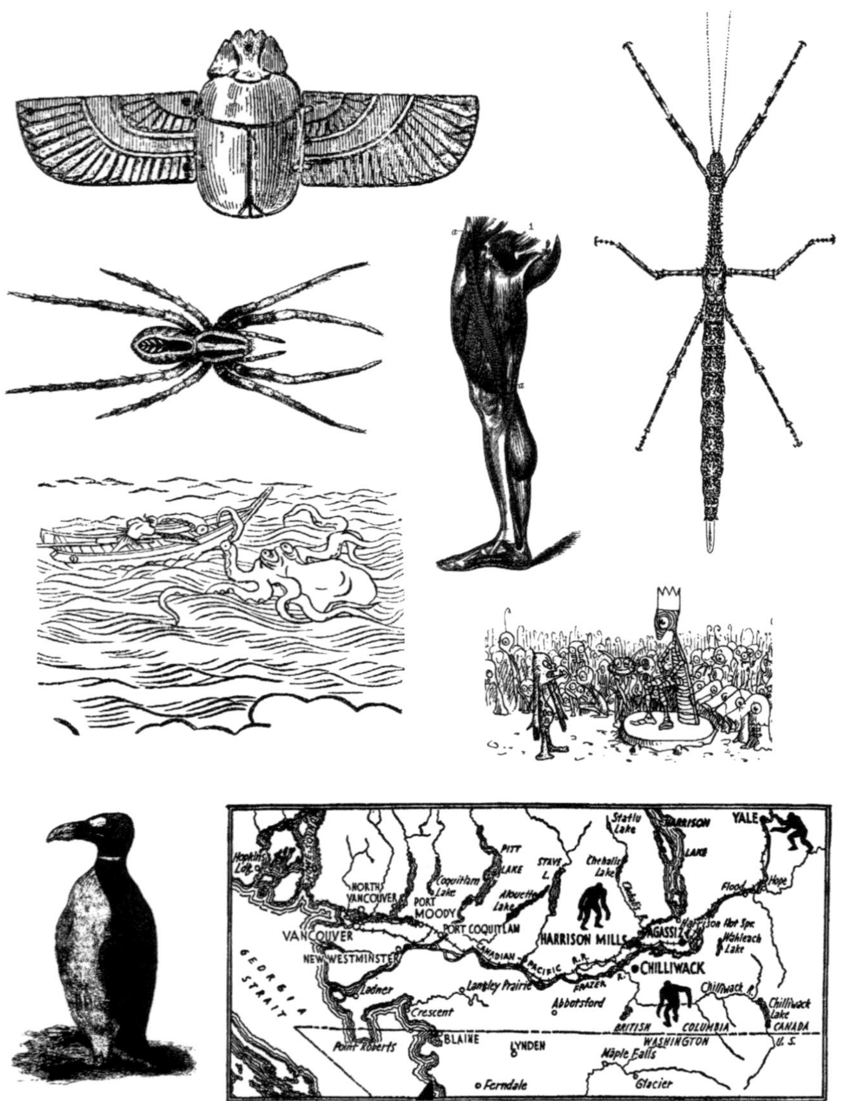

LaVergne, TN USA
16 March 2011
220301LV00001B

9781616460747